vastu vidya

The indian art of placement

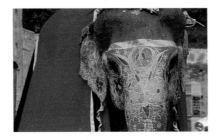

"Salutation to Ganesh"

vastu vidya

The indian art of placement

Juliet Pegrum

Gaia Books Limited

A Gaia original

Books from Gaia celebrate the vision of Gaia, the self-sustaining living Earth, and seek to help its readers live in greater personal and planetary harmony.

Editorial: Jo Godfrey Wood, Susanna Abbott
Design: Phil Gamble
Picture research: Kathy Lockley
Illustration: Mark Preston, Peter Mennem, Phil Gamble
Photography: Adrian Swift
Managing editor: Pip Morgan
Direction: Patrick Nugent
Production: Lyn Kirby
Proofreading and index: Lynn Bresler

I dedicate this book to the happiness and prosperity of all those who benefit from the ancient wisdom of Vastu

Juliet Pegrum

GAIA

® This is a Registered Trade Mark of Gaia Books Limited
Copyright © 2000 Gaia Books Limited, London
Text Copyright © 2000 by Juliet Pegrum

First published in the United Kingdom in 2000 by
Gaia Books Ltd, 66 Charlotte Street, London W1P 1LR
          and 20 High Street, Stroud, Glos GL5 1AZ
ISBN 1-85675-106-6

A catalogue record of this book is available from the British Library.
Printed and bound by Kyodo, Singapore

10 9 8 7 6 5 4 3 2 1

Foreword

Many people think that successful decorating is a matter of slapping on the latest paint colour, choosing some new curtains, and rearranging the furniture. I disagree. As an interior designer, my aim is to create living and working spaces that not only look good but feel good and function efficiently, whether their purpose is cooking, sleeping, or relaxing. This means careful thought about how a particular room will be used, what kind of person will use it, and the effects of street noise, lighting, and other external factors. So, although things such as colour and texture are important, for me they come at the end of the whole process of planning how to reinvent a kitchen, bathroom, or whatever.

That is why I was so intrigued when I first heard about Vastu Vidya, the ancient Indian art of designing and arranging buildings. What Vastu tells us is that our homes and workplaces are affected by the same forces that rule the world around us—the movement of the planets, gravity, solar energy, and so on. These hidden forces should play a central role in our choices about the kind of homes and workplaces that we want.

Juliet Pegrum gives us the tools for understanding and applying Vastu in our own lives. She guides us through the ancient myths and legends which have shaped Vastu, explains how to understand the alignment of your home or office, and suggests appropriate layouts for each room, and the best colours to use. By using the techniques she describes, we can ensure that any room is located and arranged in tune with nature's cycles and the daily activities of our life. Put simply, this means, as the old saying goes, "a place for everything and everything in its place". This makes good sense. Best of all, Vastu is practical *and* flexible, so you can easily adapt it to your own needs, whether you live in a bedsit or luxury apartment.

The practitioners of Vastu promise that it will bring health, wealth, and happiness—a result any interior designer would be proud to achieve. With Juliet Pegrum's book in our hands, we can all begin to create spaces which are efficient, comfortable, and enjoyable to live and work in. Perhaps with a renaissance of this ancient art we might embrace a new vision of homes and workplaces which nurture our minds, bodies, and spirits, instead of interiors which are fashionable but, all too often, sterile places that do nothing to meet our real needs as human beings.

Laurence Llewelyn-Bowen

Contents

The Hindu deities and Vastu

Hindu mythology contains a large pantheon of gods symbolizing various transcendent and invisible forces. Gods directly related to Vastu Vidya are derived from the *Vedas*, among the oldest literary works of mankind, possibly dating from 2500BC.

The Hindu triad of Brahma, Vishnu, and Shiva and their wives are also important to Vastu, although they are later, puranic deities. The *Puranas* are traditional stories and are later than the *Vedas*, though it is believed that none is older than the eighth century AD. Therefore they were introduced to Vastu later and probably superseded in importance older Vedic deities.

The wives most prevalent in Vastu are Lakshmi, wife of Vishnu, and Saraswati, wife of Brahma. Lakshmi, Goddess of Fortune, is often kept to attract wealth. Saraswati is Goddess of Science and Wisdom, reputed to bestow sanctity and progeny. Lord Ganesh, son of Shiva and Parvati, is one of the most popular gods, worshipped throughout India.

SHIVA/Parvati
Shiva is the creator and destroyer; the passage of time and new life created from destruction. He is usually depicted with a blue throat and his sacred animal is Nandi, the bull. He has four arms, usually holding a bow, a club, a drum, and a noose. His symbol is the *linga*, or phallus, often accompanied by the female *yoni*.

VISHNU/Lakshmi
Vishnu has ten major incarnations: Matsya, Kurma, Varcha, Narashima, Vamana, Prasurama, Rama, Krishna, Buddha, and Kalki. Vishnu began as a minor cosmic deity, but developed to make up the apex of the modern Hindu pantheon. He is often depicted with his consort Lakshmi resting on a lotus. His sacred animal is Garuda, the half-man, half-bird creature.

BRAHMA/Saraswati
Symbol of creation, connected with the origin and control of the universe, Brahma has four faces, of which only three are normally visible. These represent the four Vedas. His four hands denote the four directions and hold objects such as a rosary, water pot, book, sceptre, spoon, bow, or lotus. The swan is his vehicle.

GANESH
Ganesh has an elephant's head, four to ten arms, and a rounded belly. His vehicle is a rat and he holds a rope, an axe, a goad, and a dish of sweet balls. The fourth hand is in the boon-giving position. Known as the remover of obstacles, Ganesh is worshipped at the start of a journey or a project. He is also known as the God of Wisdom.

The Vedic deities

These gods may have been the result of the fusion of ideas brought in by migrants and those of the indigenous people, which were eventually written down in the form of the *Vedas*. Each deity was visualized as assuming human or animal form. Nirtti is both female and male, being the Goddess of Destruction and the Lord of Demons.

Soma: God of the Immortal Ambrosia

VIshwakarma: Architect of the Gods

Agni: God of Fire

Kubera: God of Wealth

Indra: King of the Gods

Yama: God of Dharma and Death

Vayu: God of Wind

Varuna: Lord of the Waters

Nirtti: Lord of Demons

Introduction

Are you looking for a new house but are overwhelmed by the wide range of options available? Are you dissatisfied with your kitchen but cannot quite pinpoint why? Are you thinking of starting a business and wondering where to locate it? Or perhaps you are about to landscape your garden but need advice. The tradition of Vastu may help answer your questions and offer valuable guidance. The advice in this book can help you to design, arrange, and organize your home and workplace, and in so doing improve good fortune and give you lasting well being.

Vastu Vidya is one of the most valuable treasures of ancient Indian knowledge. The word

Vastu means to dwell and *Vidya* means science, so Vastu Vidya is the sacred science related to designing and building houses. Vastu is rooted in Vedic philosophy, which emerged around 4,500 years ago. Many believe that Vastu is the distant ancestor of Feng Shui, the Chinese art of geomancy. Like Feng Shui, Vastu aims to restore the balance between the home (the microcosm) and the cosmos (the macrocosm), bringing health, wealth, and happiness.

According to Vastu, the external and the internal are interchangeable, for the underlying energies that govern the elements, such as wind or fire, are the same as those that control the organs

Vastu in action
Whether the home is modest (see left) or sumptuous (see opposite), the same principles of Vastu Vidya apply. The Vastu Purusha Mandala, a yantra that encapsulates all the forces acting on a given space, leaves a central area, say a courtyard, free of energy, which flows around the outside.

of the human body. However, in recent times, the essential connection between the two has been forgotten, modern humankind having dissociated itself from the fundamental forces that govern the universe. As a consequence society has become scattered and restless, alienated from the natural world. The chaos in and destruction of the earth's delicate eco-system and the rapid extinction of species are manifestations of this dichotomy. Vastu states that when buildings and forms echo the underlying cosmic principles, they become a part of the basic structure of the universe and vibrate in harmony with it. These positive vibrations have a direct effect on the inhabitants.

Vastu contains the hidden key to realigning the home with cosmic principles such as solar energy, the movement of the celestial spheres, the magnetic field of the earth, gravity, and the influence of the moon and sun. It offers a holistic approach to the design and layout of houses. Although the principles of Vastu are constrained by ancient universal laws, they are unconditioned by time and remain as relevant today as they were 4,500 years ago. Nor are they confined to a particular country, climate, or hemisphere.

Originally the wisdom of Vastu was carefully guarded, as it was considered sacred. However, because in India the home is also the place of daily worship, the principles dealing with orientation, proportion, and site planning that were applied to temples also came to be applied to the home.

In Vastu, it is understood that energy lines run like a large grid across the earth, from north to south and from east to west. Orientating living and working spaces using a compass in accord with these space directions has a direct influence on the residents. This electromagnetic field affects the human body at a vibratory level, as each single cell in the body acts like a receiver. Human consciousness also responds instinctively to the cardinal directions: the east is the direction from which the sun rises, ushering each new day, thereby representing the essence of all beginnings; the west indicates the opposite, for as the sun dims we are reminded of endings, the unknown, and darkness; the north is the direction of the Pole Star, the fixed point in the sky that denotes stability and security; the south represents the past and our ancestry. These cardinal points symbolize earth and the ground rock, from which all forms emerge.

Proportion deals with measurement, without which there can be no form. Mathematics and numbers comprise the fabric of the universe and perfect proportion reflects the perfection of the universe and brings the microcosm into conformity with the macrocosm. No building can be constructed or room properly arranged without a plan. The plan used in Vastu is the *Vastu Purusha Mandala*, a three-dimensional yantra (a diagram mapping cosmic energies) encapsulating all the forces acting on any given space. Purusha, symbolized as a man with his stomach facing earth, is the embodiment of all the cosmic forces. When his image is laid across any home, his head positioned towards the north-east, the home becomes the body of Purusha, the body of all universal energies. From the blueprint of the Mandala, any working and living situation can be properly aligned. The Mandala takes the form of a square representing the earth in its fixed aspect with the eight compass directions, for it is believed that a square plot exhibits the same qualities as the entire organism of earth.

In India, it has long been understood that health and happiness do not rely solely on things such as food or exercise. If the mind is upset, the whole body is thrown out of balance, inducing

Sunrise and sunset
As humans, we respond instinctively to the cardinal directions. Sunrise and sunset are especially important. Praying to the rising or setting sun whilst immersed in water symbolizes the merging of opposites.

illness. The energy channels of the body, or *nadis*, receive subtle cosmic energy referred to as *prana*. Vastu stipulates that if prana is functioning properly within the home, it ensures good health, wealth, and happiness. Those who ignore the advice of the *Vastu Shaastras* (rules and regulations pertaining to Vastu) will experience continual sorrow and disappointment.

The traditional wisdom of Vastu is not easily deciphered from original texts; instead, the ancestral secrets have been passed by word of mouth from master to disciple, otherwise known as "direct transmission". Through this method, the knowledge of Vastu has remained intact. I was fortunate enough to receive teachings from a practitioner, Dr Subramanya Babu. As an artist and textile designer, I have been researching the natural dyes and indigenous textile techniques of Rajasthan and Gujarat for eight years. I first heard of Vastu while developing design ideas and studying yoga in Jaipur and my curiosity was aroused. I was subsequently introduced to Dr Babu, who accepted me as his student.

The first part of this book deals with the underlying premise from which Vastu has evolved. It describes the multifarious nature of the various forces that exert an influence on any given space. Much of the traditional philosophy of Vastu is expressed in terms of myths and symbols, tools by which the mind can comprehend these hidden forces. The first section culminates in the Vastu image of an ideal home,

with each of the everyday activities assigned to different locations. However, this model portrays an idealized situation and is not a fixed formula. It is understood that every living circumstance is unique and the majority of homes do not conform to this model. This book is intended to introduce Vastu both to those who are new to home design and to others who may already be familiar with Feng Shui. However it is always advisable to consult a qualified Vastu practitioner.

Both Vastu and Feng Shui help to sharpen awareness of our immediate environment. Often we are so preoccupied with our daily lives that our perception becomes blinkered. Minor details that continually disturb us, such as a broken hinge on a cupboard door, are often overlooked, but if put right we can be spiritually uplifted.

The second part of the book outlines everyday applications of Vastu at home and work, offering practical tips on how to create a healthier and more balanced living and working environment, thus bringing contentment and prosperity. It incorporates ideas of the alignment of the home, arranging furniture in relationship to different activities and the movements of the sun, and recommends rituals and devices for removing negative influences. The science of Vastu is complete in itself and, if properly applied, will ensure happiness in worldly life. It offers a vision of the supreme truth of the energies lying behind all phenomena, reconnecting humankind to the environment and to our true nature.

PART ONE: The Origins of Vastu

Chapter one

The forces at work

What are the forces? According to Vastu Vidya an unseen force pervades the entire manifest world. Due to our confined perspective, when we think of everything in the universe, we tend to think of the material aspect: all that can be observed and measured using our five senses.

According to Hindu mythology, at the dawn of civilization the Ancient Sages, or Rishis, portrayed as semi-divine beings due to deep meditation practices and rigorous austerities, acquired the knowledge of the workings of the universe. The Rishis perceived that the foundation of the visible world lay in the invisible world, the world of spirit. In the *Mundaka Upanishad* it is described as *that which is neither tangibility, nor antecedent, colour, eyes, ears, hands, feet; of that which is prevalent everywhere, immeasurably minute, self-evident, indestructible, always alive, of that which the wise name the source.*

The idea is not far removed from modern physics. One of the fundamental laws of physics is that matter equals energy. Science now proclaims that the universe started as energy and transformed into matter, and that forms consist of tightly bound energy. It is by the effect of atomic energy vibrating at different frequencies that solid forms are perceived.

The Ancient Rishis were aware of the hidden force underlying the universe and used symbols and myth both to describe it and as a means of reconnecting to the invisible world. The image of the unseen energy is *Vastu Purusha*. Purusha is "spirit" or "essence", representing the all-pervasive life force inherent in all existence. This chapter describes the cosmic forces contained within Purusha, such as solar energy, the movement of the planets, and the earth's magnetic field, for, according to Vastu, they all influence events on earth including, on a microcosmic level, our own homes. Designing homes in accordance with these cosmic forces enhances the spirit of the environment. In homes where the structure and the energies influencing it are working in harmony, the sense of well being and peace becomes almost palpable.

The Trimurti
This is the collective title of the Hindu trinity, comprising Brahma, Vishnu, and Shiva. The Trimurti represents the three energies, the *gunas*, which underlie all manifest forms existing in the universe.

The myth of Vastu Purusha

For many thousands of years humankind has employed mythology to describe and assimilate the mysteries of the manifest universe. The word myth is derived from the Greek *muthos,* meaning "story". Myths draw together the strands of history, philosophy, and science in a narrative form, which helped the Ancients to understand the movement of the sun and the stars in the sky, the changing of the seasons and the otherwise inexplicable universal order.

Just as the mythology of the Ancients can be seen to represent real forces in fictional form, so too are the gods and divinities of Indian cosmology more than mere superstition. They are a symbolic language encapsulating transcendent and invisible forces, with each separate deity representing different aspects and elements of our manifest world. Mythology can therefore be perceived as a symbolic language, which communicates directly with our collective subconscious.

An omnipotent power

The principles of Vastu have emerged from such mythology: in the beginning there existed an entity which had neither name nor form; this nameless, formless phenomenon had such an omnipotence that it blocked out the entire sky and earth, so the gods gathered together and pressed this entity into the ground by sitting on it. At last the mighty *Brahma,* the Hindu God of Creation, gave it the form of a man with his stomach facing towards the earth, and this form became known as Vastu Purusha (pp.58-63).

Purusha in the home

In India it is taken for granted that Vastu Purusha exists in every home, with his physical posture aligned along the north-east, south-west diagonal. The head rests in the north-east and the feet and folded legs in the south-west. Everyday rituals are performed to him in the home, though never in the temple—offerings to the Goddess of Wealth are placed at his head and those to appease the divinity of time and death are put at his feet. Offerings to the creator Brahma and to the God of Architecture, *Vishwakarma,* are made to his heart at the centre.

Vulnerable points

Certain points on his body, called *Marma Sthanas,* such as the heart, are considered vulnerable or weak spots, so heavy furniture or pillars are never positioned in these areas. Blessed with divine power, Vastu Purusha rewards those who construct their homes mindfully with prosperity and power in every aspect of their lives.

Down to earth

The form of Vastu Purusha looks down on earth, offering his sacred body, with its unique energies, to help us live our lives to the full. He brings cosmic order quite literally down to earth. In the *Mundaka Upanishad* it says of Purusha that he is the innermost self of all. Fire his head; sun and moon his eyes; the four quarters his ears; revelation his voice; wind his breath; world his heart; earth his feet.

The Ancient Sages

The Ancient Sages, or Rishis, are regarded in India as the fathers of the human race. Their names are *Kasayapa, Atri, Bharadwaja, Gautama, Vismamitra, Jamadagni,* and *Vasishta.* At the beginning of time they revealed the laws of the universe, namely the basic energies that combine to create life. Seven in number, they are the authors of the Vedic Hymns. The *Vedas* are the oldest Indo-European philosophical documents, containing the foundation of Indian thought,

culture, and sacred law. These holy texts are divided into three parts: the *Samhitas*, comprising the *Rig-Veda* (songs in praise of the gods), the *Sama-Veda* (melodies accompanying these songs), and *Yayur-Veda* (sacrificial formulae); the *Brahmanas*, which explain the significance of sacrifices and rituals and how they should be performed; and the *Aranyakas* and *Upanishads*, which are philosophical and mystical writings discussing the nature of the Highest Reality. The word *Veda* is derived from the Sanskrit word *vid* meaning "to know". The *Vedas* shed the divine light of knowledge on all humanity. When exactly they were written remains unclear, although there is evidence of their existence dating back to 2500BC. The *Shilpa*, the science of art and architecture, which includes Vastu, is derived from the *Atharva-Veda* and is of later origin.

The Rishis perceived the gigantic drama of cosmic powers in opposition, with the positive and negative forces vying for supremacy. They were at one with the cosmic forces, being part of the universe and made of the same substance. They acted as mediators between the world of

The fathers of the human race

Although the Rishis are represented as human, they are considered by some to be a part of the cosmic powers and appear whenever a new universal law is needed for the progress of humanity. These seven Rishis, after leaving a great gift to humankind, were transported to the heavens, where they sit as a shining example for all to see. They constitute the seven stars in one of the brightest constellations, known as the Great Bear, the Plough, or Big Dipper.

The Rishis

The Ancient Rishis discovered the connection between all elements, identifying these characteristics in themselves. This frieze is in the Khajuraho Temples, Madhya Pradesh.

men and the world of the gods. Using meditation they transcended the narrow confines of their own individuality and explored the unending mysteries of the universe. They understood the correlation between the macrocosm, the universe, and the microcosm, the earth and human behaviour. All created forms are in some way dependent in their expression on laws outside the human realm and the Ancient Sages understood and followed these laws, which may appear to us as limiting creativity and restricting freedom.

Through their minute observations of the movement of the earth in space, the Ancients could calculate auspicious times to start building or to move house. They also formulated the technical principles behind the design of cities and houses that respected the subtle energetic or magnetic forces. Known in the Chinese system as *chi*, this energy affects the thoughts and emotions of humankind.

The heavens: the cosmic equation

Vastu Vidya is closely connected with astrology, basing many of its observances on the science of time. Astrology belongs to a branch of the *Vedas* called *Vedaanga*, one of the six sciences used as a tool for unlocking and understanding the *Vedas*. A hymn dedicated to the cosmic being illustrates the close relationship between the two: *The Vedas are his feet. The Vedic Sciences (Vedaanga) are his ornaments.*

During the fifth century AD an Indian astrologer named Aryabhatta stated that the earth orbits around the sun, though historically Copernicus has been credited with this discovery in AD1543.

The science of light

The familiar word astrology is derived from the two Greek words: *astra*, meaning "stars", and *logos,* meaning "logic". It means, literally, the doctrine or law as directed by the stars and the planets that have an influence on all human and terrestrial affairs. In Sanskrit astrology is known as *Jyothisha*, or the science of light, and is based on the evolution of time.

There are continual records of astrological knowledge dating back to 4500BC. The great astrologers of India, who first compiled and recorded the knowledge are Aryabhatta, Garga, Kalidasa, and Varahamihira. They understood the procession of the equinoxes, and the observation and precision necessary to establish such a theory continues to impress modern astronomers.

Indian astrology is also known as *Pratyaksha Shaastra*, meaning that which is visible in the apparent movements of the planets. The Ancients noted and understood how the stars and planets moving through space create a whole variety of magnetic forces that have a profound influence on human behaviour.

The study of magnetic changes

Stars and planets are manifestations of matter in space, always obeying the laws of gravitation. The atom is the smallest conceivable particle of an element, consisting of a central nucleus (containing protons and neutrons), and surrounded by electrons revolving in prescribed orbits, just as the planets orbit the sun. Being a compound of atoms the human body is affected by the gravitational pull of the planets as they move around the sun. Astrologers study these gravitational changes and the position of the planets, and interpret their influence on the lives of individuals, anticipating whether their effects will be good, bad, or indifferent.

The horoscope

The word "horoscope" is derived from the Latin *hora,* meaning "hour" and *scope*, "the watcher". The horoscope is a way of gauging the effects of the planets at any given moment and has been described as a map of man's destiny. It plays an important role in Vastu when identifying auspicious times to commence work on a house, to calculate the most favourable position for the main door or entrance, when to move in, or when to hold a house-warming ceremony. It is the horoscope of the registered owner that is always analyzed, to the extent that a Vastu practitioner may advise a client to delay moving in until the time is favourable. In some instances people have been known to wait for over three months.

An early Indian zodiac

This is an early Indian illustration (below) of the zodiac, called bhachakra in Hindi. The zodiac comprises a band of stars that forms a backdrop across which the planets move through space. The zodiac has a total span of 360°, which is divided into twelve segments of 30° each, representing the twelve calendar months, called "houses" in the West and "rashis" in India. Each segment contains an individual constellation, which is given a name of the sign of the zodiac, e.g. Aries, Gemini, etc. These are known by different names in Hindu astrology (p.24).

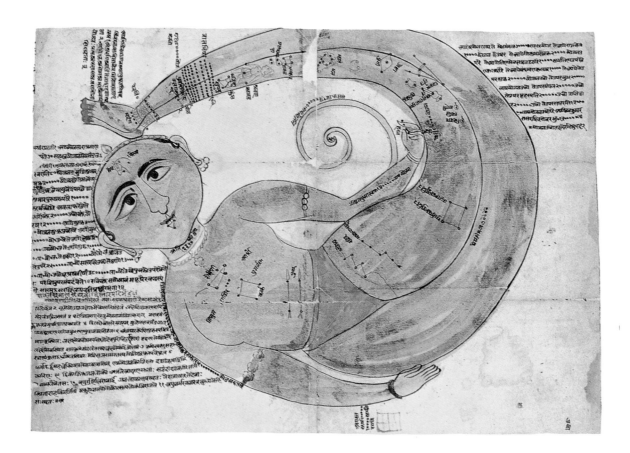

The solar system

To have a basic understanding of astrology it is important to grasp the primary concepts of astronomy and how the planets relate to one another in the solar system. Born at least 5,000 million years ago, the solar system consists of the sun and the celestial bodies that revolve around it. There are nine major planets, or *grahas*, that revolve around the sun, held in their individual orbits by its tremendous gravitational pull. Some planets have natural satellites called moons that in turn revolve around them. The planets move around the sun in paths called orbits. Their orbits are elliptical, shaped more or less like flattened circles and, with the exception of Pluto, they travel more or less on one plane.

12 **Meena** *Pisces*	1 **Mesha** *Aries*	2 **Vrishna** *Taurus*	3 **Mithuna** *Gemini*
11 **Kumbha** *Aquarius*	*The Hindu zodiac* The zodiac of 360° is divided into 12 houses, which are distinct from the signs, though analogous to the attributes of each.		4 **Karka** *Cancer*
10 **Makar** *Capricorn*			5 **Simha** *Leo*
9 **Dhanu** *Sagittarius*	8 **Vrishchika** *Scorpio*	7 **Tula** *Libra*	6 **Kanya** *Virgo*

Out of the nine planets, five were known to the Ancients and were believed to have a direct effect on terrestrial events. These, in order of increasing distance from the sun, are: Mercury, Venus, Mars, Jupiter, and Saturn. Mercury and Venus lie between the earth and the sun and are termed the minor, or interior, planets. Mars, Jupiter, and Saturn lie outside the earth's orbit and are called exterior, or superior, planets. The planets Uranus, Neptune, and Pluto were discovered more recently and, because of the enormous distance lying between them and the earth, are not considered to have a strong effect on it or its inhabitants.

The other astral body that is of great importance to the Indian astrologer is the moon, the earth's only natural satellite. It is a ball of barren rock about one-quarter of the size of earth and about 384,400 km (239,000 miles) away. The moon's orbit is not a circle but an ellipse, and it always shows the same face. It has a strong gravitational force, causing the oceans to move,

The phases of the moon
During one lunar cycle (right), varying amounts of sunlight are reflected by the moon when the entire face is lit. This is the full moon, or *Poornima*. When only a thin strip of light can be seen, this is the new moon, or *Amaavaasya*. These appearances are called "phases", and are so regular that they have been used to measure time. The phases of the moon regulate all the festivals and fasts in India, as well as accurately predicting the changes of season. The moon also marks the two starts to the year in India: *Chandramaana Yugadi* for the followers of the moon's movement and *Sauramaani Yugadi* for the followers of the sun's.

thereby creating the tides, and affecting human, animal, and plant cycles.

The growing, or waxing, period between the new and full moon is known as *Shukla Paksha* and the waning period between the full and new moon is called *Krishna Paksha*. In Vastu terms it is important to consider the phases of the moon when identifying a favourable time to put plans into action. For example, the Shukla Paksha is the best time to move house or start a new project.

Rahu and Ketu

The nodes of the moon (*Rahu* and *Ketu*), are the two points at which it crosses the ecliptic, the band of constellations, or zodiac, against which the sun appears to move. The nodes became important because ancient astrologers could use them to predict the dates of lunar and solar eclipses. A lunar eclipse is when the earth moves to a spot directly between the sun and the moon, and a solar eclipse is when the moon moves between the earth and the sun, blocking light shining on earth. The nodes were so important that they were given the status of "half planet".

In Indian astrology, the earth is at the centre of the universe and all calculations relate to this premise. The Indian system of calculation is different to the Western system, although either can be followed. Despite being different in form, both methods are distinctly similar in character.

The planets of our solar system

Western name	Hindu name
Sun	Surya
Moon	Chandra
Mercury	Budha
Venus	Shukra
Earth	Prithvi
Mars	Kuja
Jupiter	Guru
Saturn	Shani
Uranus, Neptune, Pluto	unknown to the Ancient Sages

The planets in the house

As the Ancients observed the movements of the planets in space, they noticed that their position had a subtle yet profound influence on each individual. They began to form a vivid picture of the characteristics and vibratory powers of each planet, noting the relationship of each celestial body to different aspects of daily existence and determining where the unique characteristics of each planet were located within the home. Each planet became a living being, a figure to be feared or appeased, which, if

sufficiently acknowledged, could enhance a person's daily life and ensure its smooth running.

The sun is the king of all the planets, having a purifying male energy and a stable and selfless nature. He is Lord of the East and resides in the north-east quarter of a house (see also pp.30-1). In India this area was traditionally set aside for the practice of meditation, the sun also representing the inner or true self.

The moon is the life-giving mother energy, ruler of subconscious, instinctive activities. She rules over the bathroom, a place of refreshment and renewal, and requires soft lighting. Her colours are white, light blue, and green.

Jupiter, the largest planet, known as *Guru* in India, is the remover of darkness, representing wisdom, learning, and knowledge. He is the teacher of the assembly of the gods. He resides in the study or the library and is associated with the colour yellow, a good colour for stimulating mental activities. He also watches over jewellery and treasure or valuables, which should be placed on the north side of a house or room.

Mercury, the smallest planet, is the closest to the sun and therefore the fastest. He is thought to be a messenger, being both changeable and restless. His Sanskrit name is *Budha*, derived

The moon
An important influence in life and in the home, the moon gives energy and rules all places in it that are concerned with refreshment and renewal.

Moon Chandra bathroom	Jupiter Guru study/library	Sun Surya meditation
Mercury Budha living/dining room		Venus Shukra bedroom
Saturn Shani basement/cupboard	Venus Shukra bedroom	Mars Kuja kitchen

▲ N

Location and colours
According to Vastu, the planets influence all the different spheres of human activity. This diagram indicates in which areas of the house the planets naturally reside, the ideal location of each, and the colours associated with them.

from the word *buddhi,* meaning the intellect or analytical aspect of the mind. He is at his most active in the living or dining room—sociable areas of the home where lively discussions may take place.

Venus is the brightest, most radiant planet in the sky, known as *Shukra* in India, literally meaning semen. This planet rules over the sensual side of human nature, governing romance, passion, beauty, and the arts. Its influence is felt in the bedroom and dressing room and the best colours to complement her are light blue, pink, and chrome yellow.

The red planet, Mars, or *Kuja*, which can be seen by the naked eye at night, is associated with fire and war and has an unstable, destructive nature. He resides in the south-east quarter, or *Agni*, which is the ideal location for the kitchen, guarding against the outbreak of arguments.

Of the five influential planets in Vastu Saturn, or *Shani* in Sanskrit, the planet of rules and confinement, is the furthest from the earth, the slowest-moving, and also the darkest, residing in all the dark places in a house such as cupboards and basements.

The sun

Radiating heat and light from the centre of our solar system, the sun is the source of all life on earth, whether on a physical, mental, or spiritual level. Estimated to be over 5,000,000,000 years old, the sun is an enormous ball of glowing gas, most of which is hydrogen slowly being turned into helium. This atomic fusion releases energy that permeates throughout the solar system. It produces heat, light, and a powerful electro-magnetic field, which subtly affects every aspect of our daily life. It is the vast gravitational push and pull of the sun that determines the orbit of the planets through space.

The Lord of the East

The sun is the closest image humankind has of a divinity, or "god", and as such is always depicted as a male, heroic figure, "a golden jewel of heaven", the Lord of the East, who storms across the skies in a flaming chariot drawn by seven horses, or one horse with seven heads. His Sanskrit name is *Surya*, meaning "to shine", but he is sometimes called *Savitri*, possibly the name given to him at night, in his invisible aspect.

In India the sun god represents the celestial door to immortality, the inner or true self, and the point at which the manifest unites with the unmanifest. It is the ultimate cosmic sacrifice, being made up of a fire that consumes its own substance, becoming a symbol of pure energy known as *shakti*. The absence of the sun has always provoked a great human longing for its

return: and the most auspicious of prayers in the *Rig-Veda* is the Gaayatri Mantra, which is an invocation to the Sun God, asking for his protection. There is also the famous *Surya Mandal stotra*, a section from the Indian epic *Ramayana*. This is part of an invocation to the sun made by Lord Rama at the request of Maharshi Agastya before he enters Lanka to do battle with the demon king Ravana. The Surya Mandal stotra is made up of twelve verses, or stanzas, which worship the sun's movement into the twelve houses, representing the twelve calendar months.

The movement of the sun

Orientation plays a crucial role in *Vastu Shaastra* (rules and regulations applying to Vastu Vidya). The east is the position from which the sun rises every day and therefore represents the quintessence of all beginnings, so the occupants of a building derive maximum benefit from the sun's eastern rays. In addition, the morning sun emits ultra-violet rays, which contain more light and less heat than later on in the day: ultra-violet rays trigger the production of vitamin D in the body when the bare skin is exposed to the sun; they also act as a purifier, killing germs and disease-carrying bacteria. As the sun moves towards the west it grows hotter, emitting more infra-red rays, which are detrimental to health.

It is explicitly laid down in Vastu Shaastra that more space, more doors and windows, and more

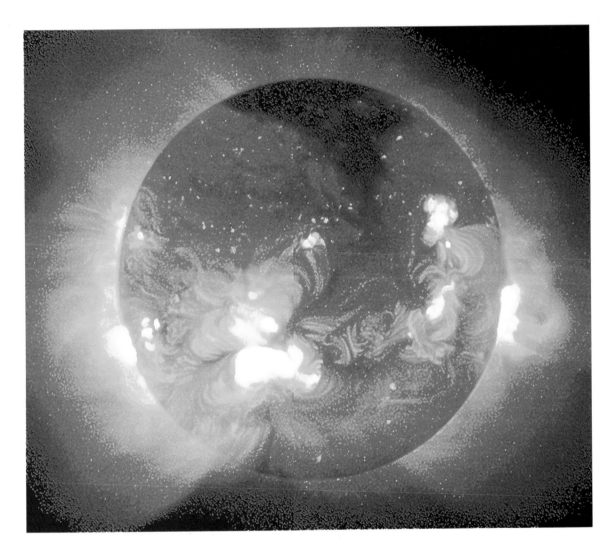

balconies and verandahs should be provided in the northern and eastern directions, so that there can be an unhindered passage for the morning rays. This means that large plants and trees, high fences, and any obstructions should be avoided in the north and east. It is even better if the ground level is lower towards the east and north.

The breath of God

The energy released by the sun in the form of solar wind is known in India as the "breath of God". It contains both negative and positive particles that filter through each individual vibrational level of the earth's atmosphere as electricity, magnetism, and light.

The earth

The earth is a huge life-sustaining globe, some 12,800 km (7,500 miles) in diameter, revolving in a relentless orbit around the sun that takes 365¼ days to complete. The earth itself spins on its own north-south axis in a cycle that takes twenty-four hours, thereby creating night and day. The third planet from the centre of the solar system, some 150 million km (94 million miles) from the sun, earth enjoys optimum levels of heat to sustain its fertile environment. Three-quarters of its surface is covered by water, which, in combination with three of the other four natural elements air, fire, and earth (pp.50-3), make life on earth possible.

A state of flux

As a living organism, the earth is in a constant state of fluctuation and change, and its well being is integral to the well being of all who inhabit it. The Ancient Sages grasped this underlying connection between individual environments and the energies of the earth and designed houses accordingly to maintain equilibrium and balance.

Delicate balance
In upsetting the delicate balance of the earth's atmosphere through mass deforestation and uncontrolled pollution, we are only destroying ourselves, for there is only one earth and no alternative ecosphere to which we can flee.

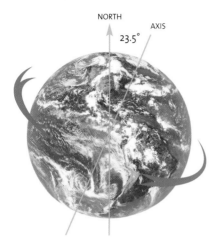

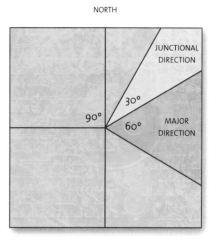

The tilt of the earth
The earth rotates on its own north-south axis, which tilts at an angle of 23.5° from the magnetic north.

Angles of the directions
The Ancients calculated that each minor or junctional direction has an angle of 30°, and that each major direction has an angle of 60°.

According to Vastu, there is an intricate system of energy lines covering the earth like a grid. These lines run from the dipolar magnetic points of north and south and from east to west, along the path of the sun. A plot of land demarcated in the shape of a square or rectangle exhibits the same characteristics in terms of the movement of energy as the entire planet earth. Using the image of the square, the Ancient Sages calculated the proportion of each compass direction. The four major compass directions of north, south, east, and west form a cross and are at a 90° angle to one another. The earth's axis tilts at an angle of 23.5°; the Ancients divided that number into 360°, which leaves an average number of 15°. Therefore an angle of 15° is taken from each corner of the major directions of 90°, totalling 60° in all, and leaving a remainder of 30°. Therefore it is

calculated that each major direction has an angle of 60° and each of the junctional directions, such as the north-east, has an angle of 30°.

Positive natural energies
By calculating the proportion of each direction the Ancient Sages were able to calculate which area of any given space the different directions influence. If properly designed and orientated the house would absorb all the positive natural energies, thus ensuring the well being and contentment of its inhabitants. With proper care and attention the design and layout of houses can echo the underlying energy patterns at work in the cosmos. The house naturally becomes a part of the fabric of the universe, vibrating in harmony with it, which ultimately benefits the entire planet.

Magnetic forces

The earth acts like a huge magnet with the dipolar points lying at the North and the South Poles. The Greeks were aware of magnetism as early as 600BC by observations of the characteristics of the lodestone, a pure or nearly pure form of magnetite rock, which is naturally magnetic. Each piece of lodestone has a pole at either end that repels the similar and opposite poles of other magnets respectively. In the first century the Chinese invented a crude compass that incorporated a lodestone, which they used for navigation. In spite of the Greek and Chinese experiments with magnetite, Western science has only identified the geomagnetic field surrounding the earth in the last few hundred years. It is now believed that the intrinsic magnetic properties of the earth have existed for at least 3,000 million years, although exactly how or why magnetic fields are produced continues to elude scientists.

A grid around the globe

The Ancient Sages of India were aware of the geomagnetic field, and believed that the electromagnetic energy of the earth forms a grid around the globe. This electromagnetic energy affects the human mind and body at a very subtle vibratory level, since the human body also displays the same characteristics as a magnet, with the head as the north pole. For this reason Vastu stipulates that you should never sleep with your head pointing north as the two similar poles will repel each other, resulting in disturbed sleep. This subtle electromagnetic energy radiates through the top of the head, the point known as the thousand-petal lotus in India, down through the spine and into the entire nervous system. By keeping this energy in balance within the body, perfect health is maintained. So buildings constructed in alignment with the geomagnetic field of the earth directly benefit the inhabitants.

Magnetic north lies approximately 11° from true north at the Earth's pole. The angle between true north and magnetic north is called the Angle of Declination. The orientation of living spaces according to Vastu is towards true north. With the beneficial rays of the morning sun entering from the east and the earth's magnetic pull to the north, the Ancient Sages of India visualized that cosmic energy is received from the north-east and moves towards the south-west. The north-eastern direction is known as *Eeshanya* in Sanskrit, meaning "purity", representing all that is good in the universe. The ancient texts pertaining to Vastu stipulate that there should be no doorways and exits in the south-west corner, for, by keeping the south-west corner blocked, the positive energy entering from the north-east will be prevented from leaving. The south-west corner of any building is known as the Preserving Zone.

Electromagnetic energy
The grid of energy around the earth has a subtle effect on the human body, radiating through the head and into the nervous system. The Rishis believed that the world and man are one reality, the same forces governing both.

Chapter two

The tools of Vastu

According to Vastu there are natural energy lines that form a grid around the planet, flowing primarily from the north-east towards the south-west, and also from the north to the south and from the east to the west. The space directions are so significant that each has a deity governing it.

Orientation is of great importance in Vastu, to assess the movement of energy through a house and to align interior components to the earth's electromagnetic field. This chapter illustrates how to harness the surrounding energy field within a space, through orientation, so as to receive maximum benefits from the cosmic forces.

In Vastu it is believed that energy movement through a four-sided structure exhibits the same characteristics as planet earth. The home, mirroring the earth, should therefore be designed accordingly. The Ancient Rishis observed that the earth's energy field is ideally balanced within a four-sided square structure, representing earth and its eight compass directions. The movement of prana (p.49) within a house or apartment flows from the north-east, meandering towards the south-east and north-west corners, before heading to the south-west. If the structure is square, energy density in the south-east and the north-west equalizes. Also explained in this chapter is the way that the square can be divided up into

zones, to illustrate how the other energies, such as the natural elements and the three *gunas*, work in the building.

The most important tool is the Vastu Purusha Mandala and this chapter culminates in a description of it, bringing all the components of Vastu under one roof. Vastu theory is a code and the Mandala provides the key to unlocking the workings of underlying energies in the universe. The Purusha is portrayed as a demon looking down on earth, with his body aligned to the north-east/south-west axis, his head in the north-east. He resides in every home as a reminder that every house behaves like a living organism. His head direction indicates that this is where the positive pranic energy enters a house, just as the air we breathe is inhaled through the mouth.

Vishwakarma: the divine architect
According to the *Rig-Veda*, Vishwakarma is the divine architect of the whole universe—the personification of the creative forces that bind heaven and earth together.

Cosmic symbols: the square

The Ancients illustrated the activities of the cosmic forces with diagrams and symbols. They perceived symbols as the secret language mapping a higher reality springing from nature itself. The first diagram is the *Sakala*, consisting of one square. The square represents the earth because sunrise and sunset, north and south demarcate the earth's surfaces. The square illustrates and unites these primary pairs of opposites, the four cardinal points north-south and east-west, and their conjunctions north-east, north-west, south-east and south-west. Orientation and space direction are two vital aspects of Vastu.

The lines

In the hands of a Vastu architect, the north-south line is the fire line, *Agni-Rekha*, with an upward direction. It represents the backbone of the universe, the *Axis Mundi*. The east-west line is the water line, which is horizontal, restful, with a feeling of expansion. The north-east and south-west diagonals are called the wind lines, *Maruta*, and create dynamic movement. These lines cross at a central point called the *Brahma Bindu*, the womb from which the entire display of forms is born. According to ancient Indian philosophy, everything in the universe—matter, mind, intellect, sense powers, names, and forms—are manifestations of one substance called *Brahman*.

The space directions, considered by the Ancients to be active forces, were expressed in the form of gods guarding the compass points.

The gods personify the laws that rule over the universe, asserting their character over human beings to influence their lives. The east is connected with *Indra*, King of the Gods. He has the highest divine attributes and is depicted riding the royal elephant. The south is associated with *Yama*, the first mortal, who transcended the other world by dying. He is known as the Destroyer and Transformer of Life, has green skin and wears red robes. The west is associated with *Varuna*, the Upholder of Universal Law, connected to fate and unexpected events. The sun is his eye and the wind his breath. *Kubera*, whose fat belly betrays his affluence, is the God of Wealth and Fame. He governs the north.

Each corner belongs to a powerful force in Vastu, being formed by the overlapping of the two facing cardinal directions; for example, the north-east is the convergence of the north and east sides. Each corner has its own character and presiding deity. The north-east is connected to *Soma*, nectar of the gods, as this is the direction from which cosmic energy naturally flows. *Agni*, God of Fire, who protects the health of the women in the house, governs the south-east. *Nirtti*, Goddess of Destruction and Lord of Demons, is connected to the south-west corner, and *Vayu*, God of Wind, rules over the north-west corner. The attributes of these gods symbolize mental and physical qualities, which manifest in the zones that they govern.

The ideal shape

According to Vastu the square is the ideal shape for a home, as the energy field present in a square structure is the most balanced and beneficial. However, it is recognized that very few structures fit this ideal prototype, yet the square diagram is still used to overlay any shaped structure to map how the space directions are affecting the building.

Dividing the square

Numbers were used by the Ancients as a means of linking the microcosm to the macrocosm and of exploring the relationship between the celestial bodies and human actions. Numbers were seen as being divine agents, with each of the nine single numbers relating to one of the nine primary planets (pp.24-7) and their respective hidden cosmic vibrations and energies.

Significant numbers

By contemplating the nine primary numbers, the Ancients were able to fathom the mysterious laws which underpinned the universe. The number nine is significant in universal law and is the number that lies beyond the manifest universe. The number eight represents nature, a combination of the three gunas (pp.44-7) and the five natural elements (pp.50-3), and nine being the next number, is beyond it.

The Sakala, consisting of one square (pp.38-9), is divided into nine equal divisions on each side to make a total of 81 smaller, identical squares (see below left). This diagram of 81 squares is called the *Paramashayika*, or the Vedic square, and is a visual form of the nine times table. Each square is numbered, although those numbers above nine with two figures are reduced to one number by adding them together (see below right). If you look at the reduced version, nine dominates as it is repeated 21 times. The Vedic square is a magic diagram relating to the planets, and is known as a yantra, a geometrical

Hindu numerology
The diagram near right shows the division of the square into the nine times table. The diagram far right shows the configuration of the numbers when those over nine are added together and reduced to a single number. Number nine becomes predominant.

1	2	3	4	5	6	7	8	9
2	4	6	8	10	12	14	16	18
3	6	9	12	15	18	21	24	27
4	8	12	16	20	24	28	32	36
5	10	15	20	25	30	35	40	45
6	12	18	24	30	36	42	48	54
7	14	21	28	35	42	49	56	63
8	16	24	32	40	48	56	64	72
9	18	27	36	45	54	63	72	81

Calculations for the Vedic square

1	2	3	4	5	6	7	8	9
2	4	6	8	1	3	5	7	9
3	6	9	3	6	9	3	6	9
4	8	3	7	2	6	1	5	9
5	1	6	2	7	3	8	4	9
6	3	9	6	3	9		3	9
7	5	3	1	8	6	4	2	9
8	7	6	5	4	3	2	1	9
9	9	9	9	9	9	9	9	9

The Vedic square

representation of energy (see also pp.86-7). Although little is known about the origin of the Vedic square, it has been used by Muslim artists and craftsmen for many hundreds of years to create fantastic geometric patterns.

Vastu practitioners use this diagram to calculate which proportion of any given space belongs to which force or direction (see pp.54-5). The 25 squares at the centre of the square do not belong to any particular space direction, but represent the heart of Vastu Purusha, the place where the god Brahma, the Ultimate Creator (p.18), resides. Of the remaining 56 outer squares, there are ten squares representing each of the major directions and four representing each conjunct direction.

Placement of furniture and room components is important in Vastu. The division of the square into the space directions is a vital diagram for the practitioner to use when designing interiors.

N

The nine sections
This diagram shows the division of the square into nine large sections. Each section represents the area of a room devoted to the specific space directions; the centre of the square remains neutral.

Key
◻ The heart of Vastu Purusha
◼ Major direction
◼ Conjunct direction

The pyramid

Provided the square base is properly aligned to the compass points, pyramids are said to possess perfect Vastu and to hold tremendous energy. They are also extremely strong structures, the square base providing a very solid, stable foundation for the triangular sides. Indeed, the great Egyptian pyramids have survived for four thousand years, weathering earthquakes, lightning, and the natural expansion and contraction of the earth. In India the triangle represents the element fire, or Agni, which is the fire of supreme sacrifice. The triangle also conveys a feeling of aspiration towards the heavens, raising the spirit of the beholder. The same is true of spires in Western churches and cathedrals.

As great resonators of energy, pyramids have remained enigmatic presences. The eight space directions converge at the Brahma Bindu, or central point (p.38), where they create a powerful confluence of magnetic energy. This energy then vibrates evenly throughout the entire structure. The great pyramids of Egypt are highly

sophisticated and abound with cosmological connections to the days of the year, the rotation of the earth, and the position of the stars and planets. In India, pyramid structures are a primeval form of sacred architecture, depicting the macrocosm, and have been present in south India since at least AD1000 and possibly much earlier. Pyramids are alluded to as a symbol of manifestation and the emergence of all forms in both the *Mahabarata* and the *Ramayana*, the great historical epic tales of Indian literature dating from 400BC–AD600. They represent the great mountains such as Mount Kailash in the Himalayas, the seat of divinity, or the mythical World Mountain called Mount Meru. Both can still be seen in south India in the form of *gopuras*.

Gopura, meaning town gate, or gateway, in Sanskrit, became very popular in south India between the thirteenth and seventeenth centuries, when they were used as gateways to great temple complexes. They are usually arranged in a series of concentric squares or rectangles and there is often one at each cardinal point. Gopuras can be built to over 30 metres (100 ft.) in height and can have as many as eleven storeys, each one of which is symbolic of the different levels or layers of realization, recording the spiritual ascent of the devotee. As you work your way to the *garbhagriham*, the heart or inner sanctum of the temple, where the image of the presiding deity is housed, the gopura becomes smaller with each separate enclosure.

Triumphant gateway
This gopura at the Meenakshi Temple, Madurai, Tamil Nadu (above) is the most spectacular feature of the site, rising to a height of 50 metres (164 ft.). Heavily decorated with sculpted figures from the Hindu pantheon, the storeys diminish in size as they rise to the sky.

Impressive structure
Brihadisvara Temple, Tanjavur, Tamil Nadu (left) is possibly one of the greatest pre-twentieth-century architectural creations in the world. This part of the structure, the *vimana*, at 60 metres (196 ft.) in height, may have been the tallest structure in South Asia at the time it was constructed. The Shiva linga housed within is considered so powerful that the entire city is influenced.

The three forces

The entire cosmic creation, which we may refer to as nature, is called *prakritti* in Sanskrit and, according to the ancient Vedic scriptures, comprises three universal attributes. These three forces are called the gunas in India, meaning a part of a whole or an intrinsic part of nature. Individually the gunas are referred to as *sattva*, *rajas*, and *tamas*. Sattva is the force of coherence, evolution, and growth, representing the creative, positive element. Tamas is the power of inertia, which leads to atrophy and dissolution, and is therefore the destructive, negative energy. Rajas typifies the energy that moves between the two extreme poles of sattva and tamas, and manifests itself as action, change, and movement.

Energies in differing proportions

Everything in the world around us is essentially an expression of these three energies, with each and every object containing different proportions of the three gunas. Thus earth is predominately tamas, while fire and water contain more rajas. No guna can exist without the presence of the other two gunas. With awareness, it is possible for a person to observe the three energies operating in their daily life by examining their alternating moods and cycles of energy. Sattva dominates in periods of joy, intelligence, and clarity. Rajas prevails during times of activity, heightened emotions, and instability, while more tamas is present when you are inactive, feeling heavy and lazy, and also during sleep. According

to the Ayurvedic system, a practice of natural healing also derived from the Vedas and as old as Vastu, each individual's inherent constitution consists of these three energies (*vata*, *pitta*, and *kapha*) in varying degrees. Because a person's nature is dependent upon the proportion of the three energies, different people respond to the world in different ways.

The three energies

In India, the three Hindu deities Vishnu, Brahma, and Shiva represent these three energies (p.8). Collectively they are known as the

The Trimurti
The collective name of the main Hindu trinity, this is a three-headed representation of Brahma, Vishnu, and Shiva, as one entity. These deities are equal in power and influence and reflect the three aspects (creation, preservation, and destruction) of the One Divine Power.

Trimurti, the three faces of God. Brahma, or rajas, creates the world; Vishnu, the form of sattva, preserves the world; and Shiva, the deity of transcendent darkness, the tamasic force, destroys it. These three oscillating, interdependent energies are symbolized by the triangle.

The ancient Vastu practitioners identified how the three gunas function within the confines of the home and how they relate to the different cardinal directions. The diagrams on pages 46-7 show the Sakala, or square, divided into four

The Three Forces

Shiva, Brahma, and Vishnu are depicted here as part of an intricate stone lintel, from the Kakatiya dynasty, twelfth century, Waragal. Shiva represents tamas, the force of destruction, Vishnu embodies the force of calm abiding and preservation called sattva, and Brahma represents rajas, the restless energy of creation.

equal sections along the north-south and east-west lines. The north-east square is the sattva portion of any given space such as a house or a room. This area should be kept as clear and uncluttered as possible because it is enhanced

The square divided in four
This diagram (right) shows the division of the square, representing any interior space, into four equal parts. Each area is ruled by one of the three gunas: the north-east corner is the positive sattvic aspect, while the south-west is the negative, tamasic, aspect. The south-east and the north-west are the two rajasic portions, oscillating between the positive and the negative poles of the north-east and the south-west directions.

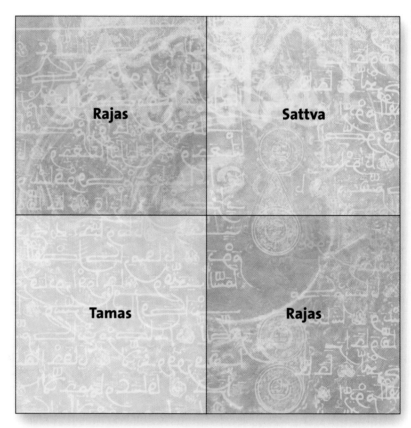

by the energy of clarity and spaciousness. The opposite direction is the south-west corner, which is the tamasic portion. This receives the least amount of light, and is therefore dark, inert, and a good location for sleeping. Tamas is also able to withstand solid, heavy weights, so this is the best area of a room to fill with large, cumbersome furniture and other heavy items. The two squares in between sattva and tamas are the south-east and the north-west squares, both of which are considered to be rajas. These areas are best for activities such as cooking, eating, or talking, so Vastu recommends that the kitchen is located in the south-east and either the sitting room or bathroom in the north-west.

If the square is divided further to take into account the minor directions (right), we can see that each of the minor conjunct directions

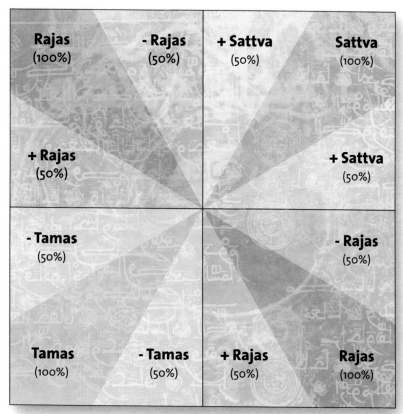

Rajas (100%)	**- Rajas** (50%)	**+ Sattva** (50%)	**Sattva** (100%)
+ Rajas (50%)			**+ Sattva** (50%)
- Tamas (50%)			**- Rajas** (50%)
Tamas (100%)	**- Tamas** (50%)	**+ Rajas** (50%)	**Rajas** (100%)

The eight compass directions and the three gunas

This diagram (left) shows the division of the square into both the eight compass directions and the three gunas, illustrating the positive and negative aspects of each space direction. For example, the north direction consists of half sattva and half rajas, the sattva portion being the more positive.

comprises the pure energy of sattva, rajas, and tamas, while the areas designated by the major directions are mixed. They each consist of two elements, one of which is more positive than the other. The north and the east are both composed of half sattva and half rajas, the sattva portion being the more beneficial of the two, while the south and the west consist of part rajas and part tamas. In this instance, it is the rajas portions that are the stronger and more positive. Throughout life a person should strive to move away from a basis of destruction towards integration and unity, which is the highest mental state. The north-east corner represents this state of being and is therefore the strongest and most positive area. Because the south-west is the furthest point away from the perfect position, it is considered to be the weakest space in a room or house.

Unified forces

Whatever exists in the universe is dependent on prana, the cosmic energy flow. The Ancients believed that if you understood the wealth of prana you could then accumulate great wealth yourself. In Chinese Feng Shui, this energy is referred to as chi. Prana is a mysterious energy: it is all-pervading yet remains unexplainable in terms of modern science, which requires chemical elements, molecules, atoms, waves, and vibrations before officially recognizing a given theory. However, prana can only be experienced in a deep state of meditation, and not with the five external sense preceptors. The opposite of prana is said to be matter, believed to be the crystallization of this

life force into perceivable elements and therefore the tangible representation of prana.

Described as the "vital breath" in the *Vedas*, prana stands for the breath of the cosmic man Purusha (pp.18-19), though it must not be confused with ordinary air, wind, or breath. It represents immortal life, for whatever exists in the universe is dependent upon it. Prana, referred to in India as the "Great, white-robed, radiant soma" dwells in the body as the "subtle" body. It is considered to be pure and taintless, as it is free from attachment to any particular form or organ, running instead as a current of energy through the 72,000 channels, or *nadis*, of the

The still centre
A courtyard in the centre of a home showing how the navel of Vastu Purusha has been left open and clear of heavy furniture and masonry. The central courtyard is a good place to relax and unwind.

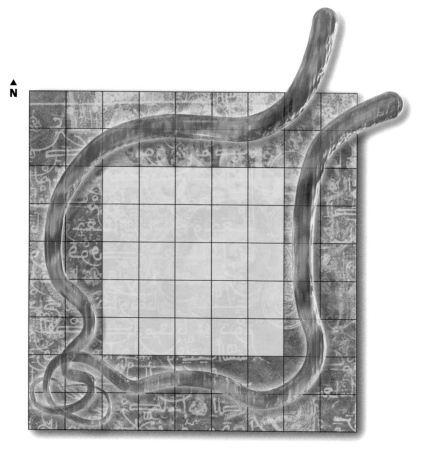

The movement of prana through a room
This diagram shows how prana progresses around a room, gently meandering from the north-east towards the south-east and the north-west before finally heading towards the south-west.

Key
■ The perimeter
☐ The domain of Brahma
▨ The flow of prana

nervous system. Prana is also known as *Asasya*, meaning "the essence of the limbs of the body", for in its absence the body would wither away.

The Ancient Sages of India studied prana and came to understand its movement and how best to harness it, noting that it flowed from the north-east to the south-west corner. They also observed that it does not flow in a straight line, instead meandering from the north-east towards the north-west and then towards the south-west, and from the north-east towards the south-east

and then towards the south-west (see diagram above). This leaves the centre of a room or a house, the navel point of Vastu Purusha, relatively unaffected by energy flow. For this reason houses in India are often constructed around an open central courtyard. Vastu Shaastra (p.30) stipulates that entrances should not be situated in the south-west corner of a house or room and that this corner should be blocked as much as possible. This is to prevent positive forces escaping, and negative forces entering.

The five elements

The five natural elements—ether, earth, air, water, and fire—are known as the *Maha Bhutas*, or Great Elements, in India. Though each one has an independent character, when they are all brought together they act upon one another in a distinctive way.

All five elements need to be present in abundance within the home to make it vibrant and filled with positive energy, and they have an interactive influence on all the various inhabitants of the house.

In Indian philosophy, the human body comprises the same five elements in the form of the five senses—hearing, touch, sight, taste, and smell. If a house is properly laid out according to the five elements, the internal energy currents in the bodies of all those living there will be normal and they will enjoy good health.

Ether

Space, or ether, makes room for all existent elements; it is the substratum for the other four, all of which depend on space to circulate freely. Space, called *Esher* in Sanskrit, corresponds to the sense of hearing in the human body. For this reason there should be pleasant and soothing sounds and calm space in the home, since too much clutter and chaos can cause stagnant energy to accumulate.

Each of the five elements is associated with a different shape, and the symbol of a diamond (see right) represents ether. The north-east section of any given building is governed by the element of ether and should be kept open and spacious to allow all the beneficial influences of the cosmic rays to enter. This is the best area for peaceful introspection, meditation, and yoga.

Air

Vayu, the Indian word for the element air, often referred to as the breath of Purusha—the cosmic man (pp.18-19)—is also given the status of a god. Vayu is the ally of Agni, as fire feeds from air. Both elements contain more of the guna rajas and have a restless quality about them. In the human body, these are represented by touch, so it is important for a house to be furnished with pleasing textures and surfaces and to have an abundance of fresh, free flowing air. The shape of the crescent moon represents air. The north-west section of any space is ruled by the elements of either air or water.

Fire

Fire, or Agni, is a predominant element within Hinduism and is deified and worshipped. The Vedic fire god symbolizes the vital spark of life within humankind, a fragment of the sun, giving life to all. Fire has the magical quality of transforming matter and accepting all substances into itself. It corresponds to sight in the human body. Within the home, lighting and colours are all-important ingredients, as well as temperature: a cold home lacks fire. Fire is depicted by the

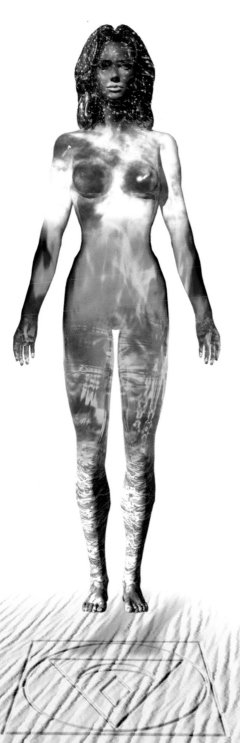

Ether
Direction: north-east
Symbol: diamond
Sense: hearing
Substance: imponderable (or light), rarified, elastic; capable of sound (vibration)

Air
Direction: north-west
Symbol: crescent moon
Sense: touch
Substance: light, cold, dry, transparent; rarified

Fire
Direction: south-east
Symbol: triangle
Sense: sight
Substance: hot, penetrative, subtle, light, dry, clear; rarified and luminous

Water
Direction: north-west
Symbol: circle
Sense: taste
Substance: liquid, viscous, cold, soft, slippery, fluid; exciting

Earth
Direction: south-west
Symbol: square
Sense: smell
Substance: heavy, rough, hard, inert, dense, opaque; exciting

The elements

Ether occupies the north-east quadrant of a building or space. Fire, or Agni, is found in the south-east quarter, the best location for the kitchen. Earth is located in the south-west corner, the best area in which to place heavy weights. Air and water are both connected to the north-west corner of a building.

Air/Water

Ether

▲ **N**

Earth

Fire

symbol of a triangle, so a building on a triangular-shaped plot should be avoided because it is akin to invoking unwelcome fire. The south-east quarter of a building is governed by the fire element and is the best location to choose for the kitchen. The kitchen was traditionally where the fire used for cooking was located, hence its position in the south-east, or fire, corner. Agni is also connected with the digestive system of the body, the internal fire, so food cooked in the

south-east direction in a home supposedly assures tasty food and keeps all the residents healthy and free from disease.

Water

Water has the same restless rajas characteristic as air, being liquid and fluid. Its symbol is a circle. Circular buildings or constructions tend to cause feelings of restlessness for the inhabitants. This is entirely appropriate for nomadic dwellings, such as the Mongolian yurt, the Inuit igloo, or the Native American teepee, but not for more permanent homes.

Taste represents the water element within the human body and is therefore closely linked to the sense of smell. In the home it represents the plumbing system of the house and all the various reflective surfaces contained within the house, such as mirrors and glass. The north-west is a good area to choose for a bathroom or guest room, since these are places where many different people may come and go without necessarily staying for long periods.

Earth

Earth represents the quality of form and is the ground on which the other three elements— water, fire, and air—function. Earth, known as *Prithvi* in India, is analogous to the sense of smell in the human body. Pleasant smells and pleasing aromas need to be present in abundance within the home. For this reason you should try to avoid living in houses located in close proximity to factories emitting noxious odours. Flowers, house plants, and other natural elements, such as ornamental twig arrangements, are also important to incorporate in the home, with the form of a square representing earth (pp.38-9).

In Vastu terms it is more beneficial if a house is either square or rectangular rather than having an irregular shape. The south-west quarter of a space is ruled by the earth element, and, because

earth has the characteristic of tolerance, this area can accept heavy weights. The south-west is the best place in a room to position heavy, cumbersome furniture and storage cupboards.

Using the elements in your home
A light and airy atmosphere is created with the help of good lighting, clean colours, freshly cut flowers to represent the element earth, a mirror to represent the water element, and a cloth to introduce pleasing textures and to stimulate the sense of touch associated with the element air.

The regents of space

The Vedic square of 81 squares, called the Paramashayika, shows the spatial influence of the eight compass directions. Each of these in turn has a presiding deity, or regent, collectively called the *Vasus*. The word *Vasu* means "that which surrounds". The Vasus symbolize the eight spheres of existence and their powers. Each regent has distinct qualities and attributes that influence different aspects of human life (pp.56-7).

The east is ruled by the god Indra, the Chief of the Vasus and King of the Gods. He is the power behind the thunderbolt and is filled with energy and electricity. Portrayed as having a fair complexion and golden skin, he rides the royal elephant. The east, according to Vastu, is the predominant direction, the starting point, with all the other points on a compass following on in a clockwise direction, mirroring the daily movement of the sun.

Agni presides over the south-east and is the Lord of Fire. He is the hidden energy within all things and has the power to bestow inner and outer illumination. Portrayed as ever-youthful, he is male and red in colour, with three flaming heads, three legs, seven arms, and a garland of fruit around his neck. He is accompanied by a ram, which he rides between the world of mortals and that of the gods.

The god Yama, Executioner of Justice and ruler of the kingdom of the ancestral dead, governs the south. He also gives his name to an ancient code of ethics in India, which is still alive today.

The sinister Nirtti, the Goddess of Destruction and Lord of Demons, presides over the south-west. In her realm belong gambling, poverty, sleep, ghosts, and night wanderers. She stands on a lion or corpse holding a javelin, shield, staff, sword, and teeth. Varuna is Regent of the West, and is depicted standing on a sea monster that is half fish and half antelope. He rules the invisible world, and is Lord of the Sea and all that is hidden and mysterious. His power is felt at night.

The north-west is ruled by Vayu, who is Lord of the Wind and the messenger of the other gods. He is the friend of Agni, whom he strengthens and helps. He is shown as a strong, powerful, light-skinned man, who rides a deer, brandishing a bow and arrow. Such is his strength that he can destroy trees and mountains with ease.

The north is governed by a deformed dwarf named Kubera, who has three legs and eight teeth. He guards precious stones and metals, and is shown adorned with ornaments and valuable jewels. He resides in the Himalayas—mountains being reservoirs of mineral wealth.

The north-east is watched over by Soma, supposedly a white milky substance produced from the soma plant. This nectar is the source of Indra's strength, the "elixir of life". Soma was an essential part of the Vedic rituals and is linked with the moon.

The centre of a space does not belong to any of the directions; instead it is ruled by Brahma, the Creator of the Universe.

The regents in daily life

The regents of space embody different aspects of daily life, and their influence can be felt in the direction of any area where they preside. The Ancient Rishis used symbols and myths to express each aspect of nature in the form of divine powers. These gods reflect the spheres of life that manifest in the directions they govern. For example, Vayu, god of the north-west, influences

Regent	Brahma	Indra	Agni	Yama
Direction	Centre	East	South-east	South
Attribute	Creator	Renewal and rebirth	Potent internal energy	Law and justice, karma
Embodiment	Balance, creativity	Fertility, wealth, children	Health, women's issues	Life and death, legal affairs
Symbol	Book (Pustaka)	Thunderbolt (Vajra)	Fire (Agni)	Club (Gada)
Stone	Ruby	Diamond	Coral	Sapphire
In the house	Central courtyard, sitting room	Children's bedroom, bathroom without toilet	Kitchen, fireplace, electrical equipment	Bedroom, bathroom, storage room

business ventures, while Kubera, god of the north, represents personal wealth. This chart outlines the direction over which each god prevails, their attributes, which area of life they influence, their symbol, associated stone, and connection to rooms and activities. For example, Nirtti, in the south-west, is nocturnal, so this is the best location for the master bedroom.

Nirtti	Varuna	Vayu	Kubera	Soma
South-west	West	North-west	North	North-east
Nocturnal deity, sleep, demons	God of Water and Rain	Lord of the Wind	Lord of Precious Stones	Immortal elixir
Fame, income, longevity	Fate, karma, fame, male issues	Communication, social life, business	Wealth, career	Knowledge, spiritual wealth
Dagger (Churi)	Lasso (Pasha)	Antelope	Mongoose (Nakula)	Vase (Kalasha)
Cat's eye	Emerald	Topaz	Pearl	Moonstone
Bedroom, bathroom, office, storage room	Living room, library, bedroom	Dining room, guest room, kitchen, bathroom	Study, library, bedroom, dressing room	Meditation room, shrine

The mandala

When all the elements discussed so far are superimposed on one another, they form a complete energetic picture, which is referred to as the *Vastu Purusha Mandala*. This is the figure of a devilish-looking man encapsulated within a square, who resides in every house, belly down, with his body aligned along the north-east/south-west axis and his head in the north-east corner. This image is not intended to be taken literally, rather figuratively, as it represents the multi-layered forces that are at work within a confined space. The boundary surrounding this space is represented by the square, even though it is understood that a house or piece of land may be irregular in shape. Vastu Purusha is portrayed as a demon to remind us that the various energy fields that surround us can be harmful if they are not properly regulated and treated with respect.

Layers working together

Knowledge of the separate layers equips the Vastu practitioner with the essential tools for aligning living and working spaces to the energy of the cosmos. No one layer is more important than another, for they all play an integral part in understanding the hidden forces at work. All the elements involved, such as water and fire, sattva and tamas, have independent characteristics. However, when they are brought together under one roof they interact in a particular way, to become a living three-dimensional yantra. Yantras are timeless charts or diagrams that map the underlying cosmic energies, which are themselves a reflection of a higher reality.

The Vastu Purusha Mandala has three components, Vastu, Purusha, and Mandala, which mirror the threefold nature of existence in terms of mind, body, and spirit. It functions on three levels: the cosmological, metaphysical, and architectural. Vastu is the canvas, Purusha is the *rupa*, or form, and Mandala is the method.

A useful grid

The Vastu Purusha Mandala provides the grid for the design of both temples and homes in order to align the microcosm with the macrocosm and secure the maximum benefit of solar radiation. The Vastu Purusha Mandala is not subject to the constraints of size, so it can be used for the design of individual buildings or for full-scale city planning. It can even be used to understand the distribution of energy in entire countries.

The earth is called *Caturbhrsti*, meaning "four cornered". This is because a square plot of land enclosed by a boundary wall exhibits the same characteristics as the earth in its entirety (pp.38-9). In the same way that the soul is contained within the physical body, the house becomes the

The Vastu Purusha Mandala
In Feng Shui the energy of the universe, or chi, is depicted as a dragon. In a similar way, Vastu Purusha is depicted as a devilish-looking demon facing down towards the earth, as a warning that these underlying energies can be harmful if they are not properly harnessed.

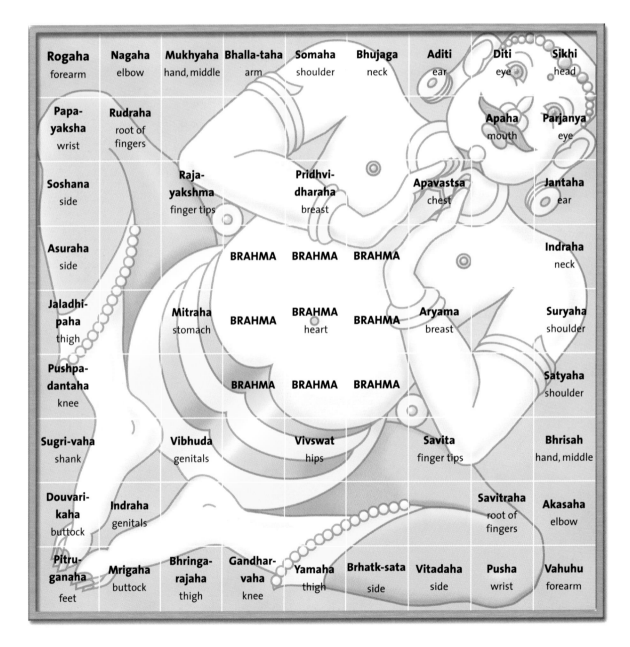

Rogaha forearm	**Nagaha** elbow	**Mukhyaha** hand, middle	**Bhalla-taha** arm	**Somaha** shoulder	**Bhujaga** neck	**Aditi** ear	**Diti** eye	**Sikhi** head
Papa-yaksha wrist	**Rudraha** root of fingers						**Apaha** mouth	**Parjanya** eye
Soshana side		**Raja-yakshma** finger tips		**Pridhvi-dharaha** breast		**Apavastsa** chest		**Jantaha** ear
Asuraha side		BRAHMA	BRAHMA	BRAHMA				**Indraha** neck
Jaladhi-paha thigh		**Mitraha** stomach	BRAHMA	**BRAHMA** heart	BRAHMA	**Aryama** breast		**Suryaha** shoulder
Pushpa-dantaha knee		BRAHMA	BRAHMA	BRAHMA				**Satyaha** shoulder
Sugri-vaha shank		**Vibhuda** genitals		**Vivswat** hips		**Savita** finger tips		**Bhrisah** hand, middle
Douvari-kaha buttock	**Indraha** genitals						**Savitraha** root of fingers	**Akasaha** elbow
Pitru-ganaha feet	**Mrigaha** buttock	**Bhringa-rajaha** thigh	**Gandhar-vaha** knee	**Yamaha** thigh	**Brhatk-sata** side	**Vitadaha** side	**Pusha** wrist	**Vahuhu** forearm

body of Purusha, who lies face down as we on earth look up at him, with his head in the north-east, his feet in the south-west, and his knees and elbows pointing to the south-east and north-west. For a building to be brought to life, each part of it has to be fully vitalized. Certain points in the house, called *Marma Sthanas*, are considered to be vulnerable, as they correspond to the heart, head, the breasts, and the navel of Vastu Purusha. Heavy weights or masonry on these points should be avoided, such as positioning the kitchen in the north-east corner, on the head of Purusha. A kitchen located in this direction is supposed to contribute to frequent sickness in the inhabitants. As it is written in the Vastu Shaastra (see p.30):

The wise must avoid tormenting his limbs with the limbs of the house, if not, sorrows innumerable will fall upon the limbs of the owner of the house.

The accumulated knowledge of Vastu Vidya has been passed directly from one initiate to the

Perfect Vastu
The Shree Swaminarayan Mandir Temple in London (near left), shows perfect Vastu. The generous stairway is white—light colours represent sattva, the highest and purest universal energy.

The 81-fold division of Vastu Purusha
As well as the division of the square into 81 (facing page) to calculate the proportion given to each compass direction, each square corresponds to an organ or limb of the body of Vastu Purusha. This diagram is useful when designing a room layout, as certain points, called Marma Sthanas, are vulnerable spots. Avoid placing heavy items on them. The central area is left free.

next. This oral tradition is called "direct transmission" in India and is believed to be the only way that a true understanding of the subject can be grasped. It cannot be deciphered from the written word alone.

Rotations

The position of Vastu Purusha above the earth, facing down (see right), is his primary position, which remains constant. However, he has two other bodies: one, called *Nitya Vastu*, which rotates every three hours. The other, which moves throughout the year, is called *Chara Vastu* and rotates in a clockwise direction, resting for three months in each position. This movement takes into account the seasonal variations in the earth's atmosphere.

Predominant directions

The movement of the sun from the northern hemisphere to the southern hemisphere affects the amount of light and heat that a house receives, and during different seasons certain directions predominate. From March until May the north predominates; from June until August the east prevails; from September until November the south predominates; and from December to February the west is prevalent. Making minor local adjustments, such as opening windows facing these particular directions during these months, is very beneficial.

The Purusha Mandala
The Purusha comprises a multi-layered system of grids, which maps the movement of energy through any given space. The image of Vastu Purusha symbolizes the cosmos, encapsulating all the energies at work within it. (See also pp.58-61.)

The three gunas
The gunas are the name given to the three energies, said to underlie all creation. Individually they are called sattva, rajas, and tamas; collectively they keep the manifest world in a state of constant flux. (See also pp.44-7.)

The 81 divisions
The division of the square into 81 smaller squares is used to calculate which proportion of any given space belongs to which of the compass directions. Each individual square also corresponds to part of the body of Vastu Purusha and must be treated accordingly. (See also pp.40-1.)

The square
Represents the earth and the foundation of existence. According to Vastu, the energies of the universe are best balanced within a square structure. (See also pp.38-9.)

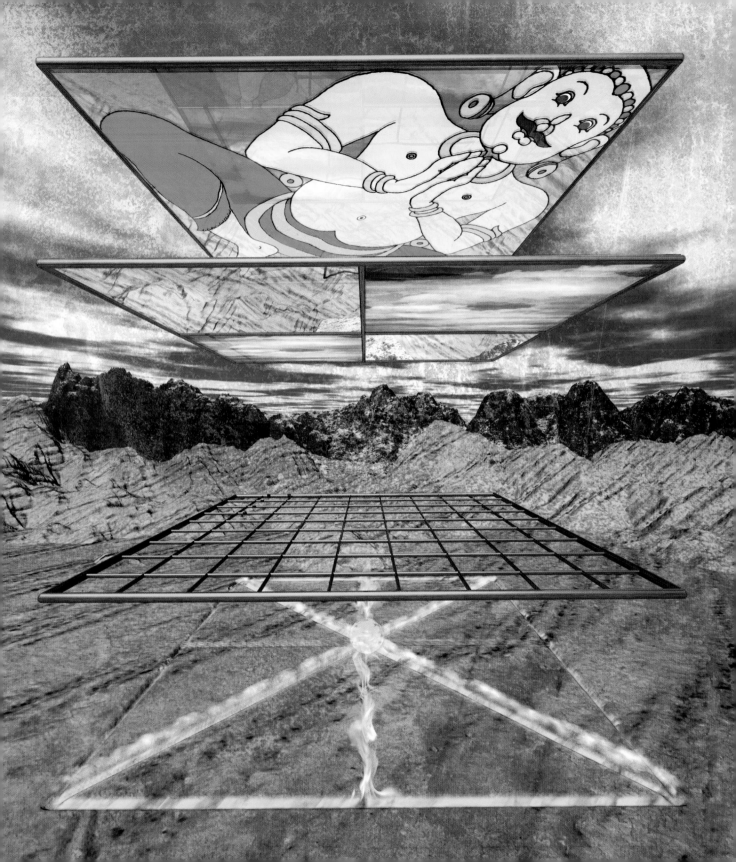

Understanding your ideal home

Traditionally Vastu has prescribed the layout of a house and the corresponding functions of each room, according to the rotation of the earth and the position of the sun throughout the day. The Ancient Sages believed that the mind and body have different activities depending on the time of the day, and designed and orientated the various components of a house to harmonize the movement of the sun and the daily human cycle.

The twenty-four hours were divided into eight, representing the eight cardinal directions. The nature of each activity reflects the quality of each direction, with the sun rising in the east, moving towards the south, and setting in the west, to highlight the different areas of the house. Houses that are not properly aligned have no sense of orientation, and can cause restlessness, misfortune, and sickness.

The period between 3 a.m. and 6 a.m., just before sunrise, is called *Brahma Muhurta*. At this time the sun is in the north-eastern section of the house. These quiet hours are ideal for yoga, meditation, or study.

From 6 a.m. until 9 a.m., the sun is in the eastern part of the house, which should be low-lying to absorb the beneficial ultra-violet rays (see also p.30). This is the time for bathing and preparing for the day, so the east is a good location for the bathroom.

The time between 9 a.m. to 12 a.m. is known as *Surya Bhagawan*, when the day properly begins and you start to feel hungry. At this time, the sun is in the south-east part of the house, which is the prime location for the kitchen. This is also the best time for preparing food to be eaten later in the day. The kitchen and the bathroom are both wet areas of the house, positioned to receive strong sunlight to keep them dry and hygienic.

After food it is time to rest, so the time between 12 a.m. to 3 p.m. is called *Vishranti*, the resting period. The sun is now in the south, the best position for a bedroom.

Between the hours of 3 p.m. to 6 p.m. is the time for studying and work, and the sun is now in the south-west section of the house—the ideal location for a study or library.

Vidya Sala is when the sun is in the west of the house. The period between 6 p.m. to 9 p.m. is the time for eating, sitting, or reading. The west is the best location for the dining or sitting room.

Traditionally the north-west of the house was where the cow shed would have been located. The time between 9 p.m. and 12 p.m., when the sun is in the north-west part of the house, was the time to attend to the animals. Modern Vastu practitioners recommend the north-west as a good location for another bedroom.

The time between 12 p.m. and 3 a.m., when the sun is in the northern section, is the time of darkness and secrecy. The north is the best place to hide treasure or valuables, to keep them protected.

This ideal layout for the house is written in the ancient Vastu texts:

Bathroom shall be in the east, south-east is the place for the kitchen, south is for the bedroom, south-west for wardrobe or dressing room, west is for the dining hall, north-west for the cow shed.
Treasury shall be in the north and Puja room in the north-east.

This ensures good distribution of solar energy.

An Indian merchant's home

Indian interiors are often painted in bright, saturated colours (left). In this Bora home, in Siddpur, Gujarat, the sitting area is decorated in a rich aqua-green. Green is a rejuvenating colour, representing harmony and balance and is often used.

Tirupati: perfect Vastu

Tirupati, in southern India, the abode of *Venkateshwara*, the Lord of Wealth, is reputed to have perfect alignment in terms of Vastu principles. It is the richest temple in India—some say in the world—receiving a staggering five billion rupees in donations a year from the 100,000 pilgrims each day.

There are three main temples at the site: Tiruchanur, Tirupati, and Tirumala. Tiruchanur

is the gateway next to the Swarnamukhi river, which leads to Tirupati. Tirupati is the largest temple complex, situated on the plains between the river and the mountains. The actual shrine to Lord Venkateshwara is located at Tirumala temple, which lies on a hill that is part of the mountain range designated as the Eastern Ghats. This is the heart of Tirupati, the peak and final destination at the end of an arduous climb. There are paths leading in from all of the four directions: east, west, north, and south.

Tirumala is the oldest temple at Tirupati, built in the mid-twelfth century during the Chola period on the site of a much older temple dedicated to the three gunas in the form of Vishnu, Shiva, and Brahma.

Surrender to higher forces

The Chola period was the time of a great renaissance in south India, with its rebirth of classical ideas and Vedic architecture. It was a period that remains very much alive in the consciousness of southern Indians today. The temple was built using Vastu principles to mirror universal truth: it was intended as a place to offer unconditional surrender to higher forces and to provide a spiritual haven to all devotees. It is popular with all branches of Hinduism.

The temple is set lower than the surrounding hills, with the highest peak to the south-west of the temple, blocking negative forces, and the lowest being towards the east. The ground slopes from the west towards the east. There is an abundance of water in the area, with many waterfalls, called sacred *tirthams*, which also flow from west to east. There is a sacred water tank to the north-east of the temple for pilgrims to bathe in called Swami Pushkarini. This has been carefully positioned so as not to cross the north-east line. The temple entrances face exactly east, while the main building lies in a south-westerly direction, with more space towards the north and east. There is a raised platform called the *mantapam*, so the south-west has been raised and is higher than the north-east. The kitchen

is positioned in the south-east corner, which is ideal for Agni, or fire. The inner sanctum, called the garbhagriham, is exactly nine hastams square (one hastam being equivalent to 40 cm, or 16 in.), with the main shrine facing east.

In its entire history this temple has never been plundered, despite military operations being carried out repeatedly within a few hours' march. In fact, while other temples suffered desecration at the hands of successive invaders, this temple always prospered from the victories of each new alien ruler.

Visiting Tirupati
Pilgrims taking refreshments by the sacred water tank at the temple of Venkateshwara, Tirupati (left).

The seven-tiered gopura (far left) above the main gateway rises into the sky as an inspiration to devotees as they enter the inner sanctum.

PART TWO: How to use Vastu

Chapter three

Vastu in your home

Vastu reminds us of the basic nexus between earth and the cosmos. The cosmic influences of solar energy, the magnetic field, the movement of prana, and other subtle energies have a vibratory effect on buildings and their occupants.

By applying the principles of Vastu to our lives, we can create a healthy environment with harmonious living and working conditions and, after years of abuse, re-establish a positive relationship with nature. This chapter shows how the philosophy and basic principles of Vastu can be applied in the home. Whatever your situation, by putting Vastu into practice you will create a harmonious balance between your external environment and your own body and mind.

Vastu is a timeless and universal system, relevant to all people at all times and not confined to the climate and conditions of India. It provides insight into the broader picture of the underlying energies and forces at work in the universe. Not everyone has the advantage of living in an ideal house with perfect alignment, so this chapter will show you how to gain maximum benefit from your particular circumstances, allowing you to remain buoyant and filled with energy. Vastu is a tool to sharpen your awareness, and will draw attention to any minor but irritating defects in your environment that have remained unnoticed and unaltered. Vastu also makes you aware of your surroundings: does your garden represent an earthly paradise or an overgrown jungle?

The principles of Vastu are applicable to any sized space and can be used on any scale, even for town planning. When we establish a home, be it a palatial residence or a one-room studio, we are creating an individual universe, a place where we can feel safe and relaxed. Each direction and area of a space naturally resonates and supports different aspects of daily life, such as eating, washing, working, and sleeping.

Saraswati

The Mother Goddess and a goddess of learning, knowledge, and wisdom, Saraswati is the patron of students and recipient of their offerings of books and pens at the beginning of classes. Her image is often seen at school gates, riding a swan or peacock, playing a vina (an Indian lute), and carrying an arrow, bell, book, bow, conch, and club, amongst other items.

Finding true north

Unless you live in a place like Manhattan, built primarily on a cardinal grid system, the compass is an essential tool. Vastu practitioners use a basic orienteering compass, which is very easy to use: lay it on a flat surface and wait until the needle stills, indicating magnetic north; align the edge of the compass, where the cardinal points are indicated, so that north sits at the point of the needle, making it possible to be correctly orientated in any space, big or small.

There is much debate concerning the accuracy of the ordinary compass. In Vastu true north is the direction towards the North Pole; however, there are only a few places on earth where the compass will point to true north, and there can be as much as a twenty-degree difference between true north and magnetic north. This depends on external influences such as magnetic storms. The Ancients practised a method called *shanku staapana* to find true north (see diagram right). Shanku means a piece of wood, otherwise known as a gnomon, while staapana means "to fix".

A gnomon is a circular stake, made of ivory, sandalwood, or some other hard wood and is approximately 45 cm (18 in.) long, 19 mm (0.75 in.) wide at the top, and 6 mm (0.25 in.) wide at

The setting sun
The compass points are of great importance in the sacred rites and ceremonies of India. Every day people flock to sacred rivers to bathe and pray. Since Hinduism advocates no one correct way, each individual carries out their own interpretation of the rituals. In this picture a devotee sits by the sacred water and makes offerings to the setting sun to ensure the sun's safe return the following day.

the base. The gnomon is fixed into flat ground at the centre of a large circle with a diameter twice its length, similar to a sundial. The large circle with the gnomon fixed vertically in the middle should be located where the *Naabhi* (navel) of Vastu Purusha is, at the centre of the site.

At sunrise and sunset or at two equal intervals before and after noon the shadow of the gnomon touches the circle at two different points, indicating east and west. Two larger circles are drawn, using their centres as the east and west points (see below). The intersection of these two circles, called the head and tail of the fish, gives the true north and south directions. The intermediate directions are located in the same way, by drawing four circles, only this time the primary compass directions are used as the centres of the circles. Where the circles overlap, they form a fish shape, which indicates the exact compass points. Appropriate adjustments are made according to the time of year and the declination of the sun.

How to find the compass points

This diagram illustrates how the compass points were originally obtained using only a wooden stake, the gnomon. This was hammered into the ground and a circle was drawn around it, using a piece of string twice the length of the height of the gnomon. Where the shadow of the gnomon touches the circle at sunrise and sunset marks the east and west directions. Two large circles are then drawn using these intersecting points as their centres. These are called the "head and tail of the fish", indicating true north and south. The intermediate directions are located by drawing four large circles using primary compass points as their centres and where the circles overlap indicates the exact compass points.

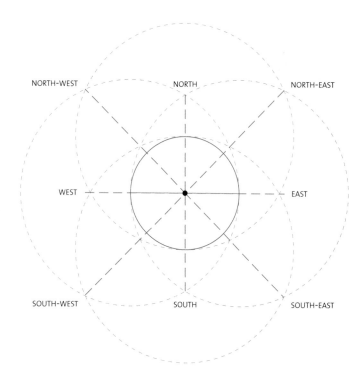

Key
- The gnomon
- ■ Shadow cast at sunrise and sunset
- ■ Initial circle drawn
- ■ Secondary circle drawn
- ■ Primary compass directions

Choosing your site

Vastu starts from the road, so the nature of a site can be determined by the direction of the road or roads that border it and is referred to as a north- or south-facing plot.

Sites with two roads bordering the property are known as "corner sites". It is very important that the corners of these sites are neither rounded nor cut across.

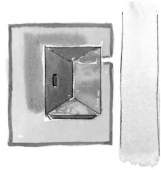

A south-facing site
A site with a road to the south can cause problems. It needs special attention from a Vastu practitioner, especially if the road is at a lower level than the house.

A west-facing site
In this example the road is to the west, thereby blocking the north and east. This site is considered neutral.

An east-facing site
The road lies to the east side of this property. It is a positive location, as the east will be unobstructed by other properties, allowing the morning sun to penetrate the site.

A north-facing site
This example shows a property with a road running along the north. Having the north side unobstructed for the free flow of cosmic energy is also positive.

A south-eastern facing site

If there is a road to the south and a road to the east, this is referred to as a south-eastern site. South-eastern properties are well located and are especially good sites for women's organizations.

A south-western facing site

This site shows a road to the south and another to the west. According to Vastu the south-west should be blocked, but in this situation the south-west is vulnerable to negative influences. This is a bad residential site, although it could be good for business purposes. If the roads are lower than the site, this can cause ill health, accidents, and criminal activities, and should be avoided.

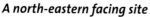

A north-eastern facing site

A property that has two roads bordering it, one to the north and one to the east, is called a north-eastern site. If the two roads are lower than the property, or on the same level, then this is considered the best possible site. If the roads are higher than the building, this will indicate possible financial problems or problems with fertility for the occupants.

A north-western facing site

A north-western site is one with a road in the west and another in the north and is considered neutral.

The lie of the land

In ancient India, to create a dwelling, a place to live, was symbolic of creating a universe. It was the earthly womb, where one should feel safe and secure, protected from harmful forces. In Vastu, every aspect of a potential living space is carefully inspected, starting with the surrounding landscape and the shape of the site.

The square and rectangle are considered the perfect shapes in which to dwell, whether it is the shape of the building or of the surrounding land, though ideally both, as the energy field present in a square, and to a lesser extent in a rectangle, are the most harmonious and beneficial. Irregular

shapes of any kind are best avoided, unless they extend towards the north-east. If, however, your garden shape is irregular, then this can be remedied by constructing a wall or hedge to square up the site. The extra portion can then be used as a separate area, as long as the area surrounding the house has been squared off.

Triangular sites

Triangular-shaped sites should be avoided at all costs: triangles are associated with Agni, or fire, so it is best not to invite its influence. Vertical triangular forms that rise from a square base are

dynamic and powerful structures and can be good for business, but not as homes. It is preferable if the site is flat, neither humped like a tortoise nor concaved. The only exception is if the contour of the surrounding land gently inclines, sloping either from the west towards the east or from the south towards the north, so that the north-east is the lowest point. A hill to the south or west of a building is fine, but never purchase a property with a hill on the north-east side: there will be no positive sunlight and your prosperity will be blocked. Natural water nearby is auspicious, although it is better if it is flowing from either the south or the west towards the east or the north.

Vastu stipulates avoiding buildings near burial grounds, sites where murder has occurred, or buildings formerly used as brothels. Also, living surrounded by roads may make you feel insecure.

Living in a shadow
Avoid buildings that are overshadowed by much larger structures such as industrial towers (above), a flyover, or a large tree. It is also worth checking air quality and rejecting a site that smells unpleasant in any way, particularly locations that are near to factories and industrial sites.

Restlessness
Circular shapes correspond to water and will cause restlessness, so are ideal for activity, such as sports (facing page). A Buddhist stupa will draw you towards movement, to circumambulate, but not to rest.

Rows of houses

As a rule, Vastu favours houses that have some space between each other. Although rows of houses may be economical and spatially more viable in a condensed city, they are considered a disadvantage in terms of Vastu, as attached housing inhibits the flow of light, ventilation, and cosmic energy.

Terraced houses that have a front garden, no matter how small, are preferable to those whose front doors open directly on to the street, as the garden area allows for the movement of prana. Ideally, the garden should be either a square or a rectangle with a garden gate positioned in a positive direction to enhance the benefits of Vastu. Avoid having a tree in the front garden that is taller than the house.

Positive and negative influences

Usually one row of houses will have all the positive influences, while the houses on the opposite side of the street will attract all the negative energies. However, those houses at the end of the row may be at an advantage, especially if the south side is attached or blocked.

Semi-detached houses are preferable to terraced houses in terms of harmonious living, although the person living in the side attached to its sister house on the south is in a better position than their neighbour.

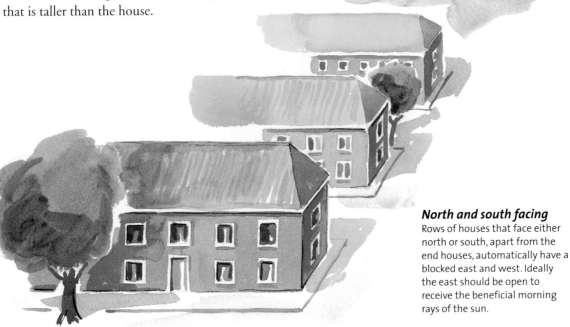

North and south facing
Rows of houses that face either north or south, apart from the end houses, automatically have a blocked east and west. Ideally the east should be open to receive the beneficial morning rays of the sun.

Benefits

The illustrations on these pages show rows of houses, facing north and south (see left), and west and east (see below). The row that faces north acquires all the benefits, while the one facing south is left with all the negative influences. However, the rows facing the east and the west are both in more favourable situations as the west-facing houses remain neutral, while the east-facing houses are positive.

In a situation where there are rows of houses opposite one another, it is important to avoid gates and doors being in direct alignment, though it must be kept in mind that the south-facing houses can be made to reap good results when handled correctly.

Terraced houses, Berkshire, England
Whichever way terraced houses face, they are renowned for fostering a good balance between individual privacy and a sense of neighbourhood and community.

East and west facing
Rows of houses that face either east or west are more favourably positioned as the south is automatically blocked. The west-facing houses are considered to be neutral, while those facing east are positive.

Apartment blocks

In densely populated cities, such as New York and Hong Kong, living in apartment blocks that are crammed together is unavoidable due to the high cost of land and limited space available. Vastu regards each apartment as an independent unit, so that the same principles of orientation apply whether you live high up or lower down.

If you live in an apartment block it is advisable to choose the first floor, or higher, to avoid the negative influences of obstructions at ground level. It is preferable if the entire block is either square or rectangular, to maintain a strong connection to the earth, even if the apartment is very high up. According to Vastu, square buildings are considered masculine, while rectangular buildings are feminine and softer. The best position for the apartment is on the north, north-east, or east side of the block, to receive the positively charged morning light. An apartment on the north-east side will also ensure that the south-west is obstructed by other apartments, keeping negative forces from entering. The block should have space around it and not be too close to other apartment buildings, so that it is well ventilated and daylight can penetrate the rooms unobstructed. Particular care should be taken to

avoid apartments that are overshadowed by a much larger neighbouring building.

The tradition of Vastu sets strict guidelines for suitable building materials to be used for construction. Ancient Vastu practitioners believed that every substance has a living energy, with some materials transmitting positive and others negative energy. Certain rocks, such as sandstone and marble, are considered to have a very positive influence on the inhabitants, while others, such as granite and quartz, constrict the flow of blood in the vessels and cause health problems. The ideal apartment block should be made from either brick or stone, not glass or reinforced concrete.

Materials

The ancient texts even specify the quality of the stone that should be used, for rocks, like trees, are thought to age and have gender. Vastu advocates the use of mature stone, which vibrates with a deep sound when struck. It feels cool and glows, while younger stone is rough and streaked. Brick ideally should be red, well proportioned, free from cracks, and resonate harmoniously.

Modern building regulations encourage the use of reinforced concrete, steel, glass, or other synthetic materials. However, they may be strengthening the building at the expense of health: modern Vastu practitioners believe that concrete is a dead material that emits a negative energy. If exposed to this energy over a period of time, people become susceptible to disease and

illness. Similarly, using steel girders in a building that is not properly earthed is like living in a huge magnet. This too causes stress on those inside.

City skyline
Cities can sometimes seem to be overwhelming in scale (left), but Vastu can help us to live life on a human scale.

Apartment blocks
In Vastu each apartment is an independent unit (below), so that the same principles of orientation apply to each individual floor.

Shapes

Irregular-shaped buildings or rooms are those where any of the corners deviate from a 90° angle to form either an oblong or a rhombus. An irregular-shaped property with an extended corner may have two right angles, one obtuse angle and one acute angle (see below left). The acute angle is always the point of extension. However, there are a few exceptions: if the north-east corner has an angle of less than 90°, it is extended, attracting positive energy. One or both sides of the north-east corner may be extended, this being the only corner that can be extended fully (see below centre).

The south-west corner may be extended to produce an angle of less than 90°, which will also have a positive effect on the inhabitants, has an acute or extended north-west corner and an obtuse south-west corner. This is positive, inspiring success on a personal or corporate level. The diagram below right shows a room with an extension at the south-east corner so that the south-west angle is obtuse. This will encourage harmony and health, particularly among the females of the family.

The Flatiron Building, New York

This famous building (right) is a good example of an irregular-shaped building. The site is triangular, representing fire. Vastu practitioners do not recommend "playing with fire", unless it is handled with care.

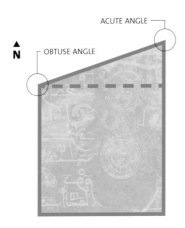

ACUTE ANGLE

▲
N ┌ OBTUSE ANGLE

Extended north-east corner
The north side of the north-east corner is extended, which is a positive attribute for the house.

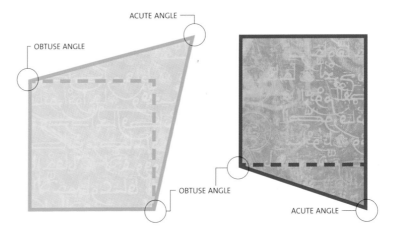

ACUTE ANGLE

OBTUSE ANGLE

OBTUSE ANGLE

ACUTE ANGLE

Extended north-east corner, both sides extended
The north-east corner is fully extended towards east and north.

Extended south-east corner
Extending the south of the south-east corner has a positive effect on the health and harmony of the females of the house.

Extensions

The square represents the universe in microcosm and, according to Vastu, is the perfect shape in which to live. This principle applies to all spaces, whether the shape of a single room or of the entire house. The square is a strong, stable shape offering maximum protection from the external elements. In this modern and diverse world, however, not all buildings and structures conform to Vastu precepts. In Vastu certain irregularities are considered to be beneficial while others are detrimental to the welfare of the occupants. Even seemingly minor irregularities, such as strangely shaped alcoves, small recesses in a room, or a

connecting area of the house, can have a significant impact on the fortunes and lives of the inhabitants.

If you are considering an extension to your current home, then it is worth knowing the pitfalls before drawing up the plans. The most important factor is the direction in which the room or building is extended: certain directions have positive effects and others negative, so it is advisable to rectify any negative extensions. The preferable shape for an extension is either a square or a rectangle. Depending on the amount of land surrounding a building, additions or extensions

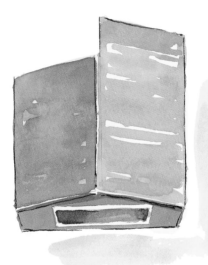

North-east extension
This extension, either in a room or a house, is always considered auspicious, attracting increased prosperity and progeny.

North-west extension
The west side of the north-west corner is extended, which is positive, improving social activities and the success of business ventures.

in the north-east section of the property are positive (see facing page, left). A north-east wing can in fact attract increased wealth and prosperity or even bring fame to the occupants. The only other directions that are considered positive are south of south-east (see below left) and west of north-west (see facing page, right).

If the south-west corner extends, this could bring with it unbearable difficulties and certainly requires rethinking. If the building is extended in the south-west corner, then squaring it, such as by adding a conservatory (see below right), can rectify the problem. The same principle applies if

the building has two extended corners creating a U-shape. If a room is L-shaped, with an extension in the south-west, you should set up a screen or partition so that there are two separate spaces. If an alcove has been extended, then block it by building a shelving unit or fitted cupboard.

If east of south-east is extended, it can cause arguments with the neighbours or among the females of the house. An extension in the north of north-west may create mental or emotional instability for the occupants.

South-east extension
The south of the south-east corner is extended, which has a similar consequence as the diagram on p.82 (bottom right), having a positive influence on the health and harmony of the females of the house.

South-west extension
This extension should always be avoided. In such cases it is advisable to rectify the situation by adding a conservatory to square off the shape of the building.

First impressions: the gateway

The gateway is the first contact that you have with a home, be it a garden gate or the front entrance to an apartment block. It is also the first impression that an outsider has of a building and a home and will influence the overall atmosphere of the place. The various cardinal points were believed to have different effects on the occupants. Traditional houses in India were classified and named according to the cardinal point they faced.

Shiva yantra
This yantra, invoking Shiva, the deity who has the power to both create and destroy life, can be used to help ward off misfortune. It is particularly effective when positioned in a south-facing direction.

To have a lower ground level with more doors and windows in the north-east quarter is always considered auspicious, not only in terms of the optimum benefits of the morning light.

A door facing east brings fame, strength, and the fulfilment of the occupants' dreams, while a door facing the north ensures good fortune and fertility. However, not everyone can be so fortunate as to have their house facing north or east. If the road is to the west, then the best position for the gate is between west and north-west. If the road is to the south, then the best place to enter is between the south and the south-east corner.

The position of the front door in relation to the gate or main entrance is important: it is preferable to have the front door of the house or the apartment facing the same direction as the gate to gain the corresponding benefits of the cardinal point. Alternatively, it is good for the house to be located on the left-hand side when passing through the gate. It is unlucky to have the house on the right-hand side when entering the gate or to have the front door on the opposite side from the gate. The reason for entering a house from right to left, is that the ground forces in the northern hemisphere move in a clockwise direction and counterclockwise in the southern hemisphere.

Vastu Shaastra also points out the avoidance of vedhas, as they restrict the flow of energy. Any obstruction is a vedha: a tree too close to the front gate, an awkward corner, a ditch, or a lamp post. A church or cemetery opposite the main gate is also considered a vedha. Naturally, it is difficult to avoid every obstruction in a crowded city, so in such cases a little distance between the door and the vedha is advisable.

A road pointing directly towards the property also creates problems and is called *veedhi shola* in Vastu. *Veedhi* means road and *shola* means arrow, so it is like an arrow pointing straight at the house. In such circumstances, it is better to position the gate so that it is not in direct alignment to the road. Failing that, you should fix a yantra to the gate and, if possible, keep a night-light over it. A yantra is a magic symbol or diagram that wards off harmful effects and is designed specially by a Vastu practitioner (see the illustrations).

Protective yantras are widely used in India. Many families grow a tulsi plant in front of their houses, commonly known in the West as basil. Sometimes people paint an image of the plant on the wall beside the door rather than grow a real one—the effect is the same (see the photograph on page 10). This aromatic herb is never used as a condiment in India, as it is believed to possess sacred properties to ward off negative energies and is therefore treated with reverence. Even the mud from the base of the plant is deemed potent enough to ward off negative forces. Supposedly, the breeze that wafts through its leaves has an antiseptic effect; indeed, basil is thought to

possess strong medicinal properties: when crushed the leaves make a good potion for the blood and, if applied to the skin, will cure irritations and eruptions.

The elephant-headed god, Ganesh, is a very popular protective amulet. He has the power to remove all obstacles and is keeper of house and home. Try keeping a figure of Ganesh above your front door, especially if the door is positioned in the south-west of the house.

Durga yantra
Durga is a powerful protection deity, one of the angry and aggressive aspects of the goddess Shakti, whose role is to fight and get the better of demons. She displays her destructive aspect in the face of disruptive forces.

On the threshold: paths & front doors

Pathways

Having passed through the gateway, you often have to walk up a path before you reach the front door of a house. A path has a surprising impact on the flow of energy leading to the house. You should be aware of any obstructions along the side, such as large stones or bushes hanging over it, and, if possible, remove them. If the path lies to the north-east, it should be broader and more open at the gate and become narrower as it approaches the house. Conversely, if the path is located in the south-east quarter, it is better that it meanders up to the front door and is of the same width throughout. Keeping a yantra fixed

to the gate or main door to ward off any negative forces entering from the south is advisable in this instance. Gently curving horseshoe drives are good, allowing for easy access and flow.

Entrances and front doors

The front door is considered to be the mouth of Purusha. As the mouth is the largest orifice of the human body the front door should be the largest door in the home. A single front door is better if it faces north or east, with steps leading up to it. However, the main door should never be placed in the centre of a wall otherwise it is believed that the whole family will perish. Ideally, it should be

Ganesh at entrances
Ganesh is honoured at the beginnings of all new ventures, particularly moving to a new house, where his image is often seen over doors and at gateways. He guarantees prosperity and progress. Because he represents the merging of the small (man) with the great (elephant), he blends the microcosm with the macrocosm.

placed more towards the north-east corner. If the front door faces south or west, it is better to have it at ground level.

No two doors to different houses or apartments should be directly opposite one another: the combination of cosmic energy and air will irritate anyone in the area, so there may be confrontation and unrest between the neighbours. This also applies to doors of different rooms within the house, as unrest may arise in either room. If your house has this problem, then you should remove one of the doors to create a smooth passage for the flow of energy.

If you are thinking of buying or renting a new home, you should ensure that the size of the door is proportionate to the house or apartment. Proportion, referred to as *maana* in Vastu, is the third basic principle of Vedic architecture, without which there are no auspicious results:

When the house is built in strict adherence to the proportionate measurements then the house becomes the abode of the gods. Mayamata

Symmetry and proportion are considered essential to the elegance and beauty of a building, and their correct application will attract and radiate a positive atmosphere. You can gauge the impression that your front door creates by measuring its proportions: if the height is equal to the width, then it conveys peace; if the height is one and a quarter times the width, it transmits

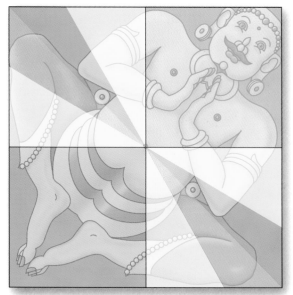

Positive entrances
These are indicated by the colour green. The south of the south-east corner and the west of the north-west corner are thought to be moving in the direction of north-east and are therefore considered positive.

Moderate entrances
These are indicated by the colour yellow and are considered to be neutral locations for doorways.

Negative entrances
Red shows negative entrances, as they allow movement of negative energy. The east side of the south-east corner and the north side of the north-west corner are both moving towards the south-west and are negative.

strength and emanates wealth; if the height is one and a half times the width, then it is joyful; a door that is one and three quarters times the width attracts wealth; and one that is twice the height of the width is considered to be marvellous in every way possible. The ideal height for a domestic door is for the height to be approximately three times its width.

Door function

The next aspect to watch out for is how the door functions: a door should open smoothly and be square on its hinges, with no obstacles behind it, otherwise it is predicted that enemies will bring ruin and destruction to the family. The best door to have is one that stays exactly where it is put: one that swings will bring misery. If the door makes a tuneful sound like a flute or trumpet when it is opened, then this is considered positive. If, however, like the squeaking doors of old horror movies, it makes the sound of a cry or an inarticulate noise like someone clearing their throat, then this does not bode well. The front door should feel solid and be made of good-quality materials, preferably wood, not metal: metal creates a saturnine influence and you will feel confined and weighed down by it.

How many doorways do we pass through every day? Doorways are so mundane that one rarely observes the effect that a stuck or squeaky door has on our psyche. Whatever the cause, whether there is a folded piece of carpet obstructing the

door or a coat rack just behind preventing the door from fully opening, all these minor defects restrict the free-flow of energy in our daily lives.

Try to be aware of what your front door opens on to: to open the door and see a friendly object, like a bookcase or wooden cupboard, is inviting and welcoming. Equally, what presents itself to you when you open the door to leave the house? Are you greeted by the bright morning light or are you overwhelmed by the shadows of trees and climbers? It is considered unlucky if their shadows cut across the front door.

The diagram on the previous page shows all the possible locations for a doorway. Each point is given a name and has very specific consequences associated with it. The same principle of positioning applies, whether it is the garden gate, the front door, or a door into an individual room. The main influence on the property or the character of a room is dependent upon its entrance. Do not despair if you find that your front door is positioned in the south-west corner of the building. There are remedies to neutralize the effect (p.131).

The position of doors and entrances, their proportions and any obstructions is an essential aspect of Vastu Shaastra. It is believed that in every direction there are exalted or positive directions and debilitated or negative directions. It is thought to be more auspicious if the total number of doors in the house is even.

The doorway

In Vastu a plain front door is considered unlucky. Evidence of this can be seen in buildings throughout India, regardless of when they were built or of their religious inspiration. Auspicious images, such as flowers, animals, leaves, and birds, are carved into the door and its frame. Lakshmi, the Goddess of Wealth and Good Fortune, is a popular image, and is usually depicted as being bathed by two elephants. In the West we might not want to opt for such intricate decoration, but it is worth looking for doorways with pleasing decorative features.

Inviting the spirits

In India, all dwelling spaces are considered to be alive with unseen entities, so certain rituals are considered essential to the success and purification of a place. There are four main rituals, or *pujas*, connected with a house: the first is performed before building actually commences; the second on positioning the main door.

Once the building has been completed it is consecrated with a third ritual to ensure that the new occupants have happy and successful lives there. This is performed before they move in and includes a ritual to rid the site of any unseen evil spirits and astral characters of animals and humans, which can cause unholy vibrations. In India it is believed that such spirits may have been using the vacant space as a permanent abode or as a meeting place for some time, so during a ritual called *Balidaana*, these spirits are asked to leave before the new protective spirits are invited to enter:

The spirits, gods and demons depart! They leave this place and go elsewhere for I take possession.

The fourth set of rituals are associated with moving in. Such rituals connected with architecture and related to how you should enter a new home are found in the *Puranas* and the *Tantras*, ancient Indian texts. Before entering a new home, a Vastu puja is performed to the imaginary Vastu Purusha, who resides in every property. Ideally a priest or Vastu practitioner should perform this ritual. First the place must be cleaned thoroughly. It is good to use salt water for

this purpose, and particular care must be taken over the floors. An invocation can be made before entering the property while holding a lighted torch or a candle:

Facing you, o house, who are facing me,
I approach you peacefully: sacred fire and water
are within, the main doors to cosmic order.

ATHARVA-VEDA

The candle is carried to the centre of the house or main room, where a jug of water, white flowers, and burning incense have previously been placed. In India, milk is often boiled as a sacrifice until it overflows or food is cooked and offered to the gods. After this, a prayer is recited for a prosperous home, free from disease, and full of wealth and happiness:

From the eastern direction I summon a blessing
to the glory of this house. Praise to the gods, the
praiseworthy, forever and ever!

From the southern direction, from the western
direction, from the northern direction, from the
depths below, from the heights above, I summon
a blessing to the glory of this house. Praise to
the gods the praise worthy forever and ever.

ATHARVA-VEDA

Finally holy water, either brought from a sacred spring or water blessed and mixed with sandalwood oil, is sprinkled into each corner of the property for purification. Then the cooked food, which has first been offered to the gods of the different space directions, is distributed to all the guests. This is called *Prasad*, sanctified or

blessed food. The five essential items required for the performance of a puja, or ritual, are water or milk, incense, flowers, a lighted candle, and a bell to represent the five earthly elements. The water or milk represents the element water, the incense, with its rising smoke, is symbolic of the element air, the flower represents earth, the lighted candle symbolizes fire, and the sound of the bell represents ether, or space. Therefore all the elements are brought together, collectively representing the entire planet earth and are offered to the gods of the space directions to ensure their protection in the home.

It seems likely that similar rituals took place in the West, where the tradition of a house-warming party continues to be popular—the link to our own ancient history.

The power of colour

Sound, heat, light, and magnetism are all part of the energy of the sun. Sunlight is apparently pure, white light, though it is actually a combination of the seven colours of the rainbow: violet, indigo, blue, green, yellow, orange, and red. This is referred to as "VIBGYOR" in India.

Heliotherapy, the use of sunlight in the treatment of diseases, has been known in India for thousands of years. The ancients also realized that each colour had an independent vibration that affected the mind and body, and activated human glands and bodily functions. The north-east side of the spectrum, which is given the name *Eeshanya* and corresponds to the ultra-violet, violet, indigo, and blue end of the spectrum, is associated with purity and divinity. The south-west corner of the spectrum is called *Aagneya* and is the infra-red, thermal aspect. Green is neutral.

Colour as a tool

Colours perpetually surround us and have a powerful impact on our state of mind. The use of colour in house decoration is a very powerful tool for Vastu, balancing the environment, both mentally and physically. The colours are also linked with the three gunas: sattva, rajas, and tamas (pp.44-7). Blue, green, white, and light colours are considered sattvic. Rajasic colours are the bright fiery reds, oranges, and pinks, and are thought to increase desire. The inert, tamasic, colours are all dark: browns, navy, and black. These colours are best avoided as they tend to make you feel inert and lazy.

It is widely known that, visually, colours can change the size and shape of a room. In a small room, a light colour gives the illusion of space. Also, if a room receives little daylight, painting it a light colour will improve it dramatically. If a room receives a lot of light, it is not advisable to paint the walls peach or yellow, though it is good to have the ceiling white as this will reflect more heat and light into the room. An entirely white room is not a good idea, as it is a colour that

Colour through the day
Morning sun emits positive ultra-violet rays represented by blue-violet. As it reaches its zenith it emits ultra-red rays represented by red-yellow. Green remains neutral.

cannot be endured for long periods, being a combination of all seven rays. In India, white is used for mourning and is associated with death. The general rule is to use softer, lighter, more sattvic colours throughout the house to promote harmony. Red is a passionate shade and, as it increases desire, is a good colour for the bedroom. It is also a good colour to use in the kitchen, whether you use red earthenware tiles on the floor or paint the walls a shade of red.

Blue and green, nature's tonics, are cooling and soothing, giving calm and peaceful vibrations, and are best utilized in the living room. Yellow is supposed to stimulate the nervous system and cerebral activities, so its prime use would be in the study or a room where mental pursuits take place, such as a library. Violet is said to enhance introspection and disperse depression, and is good to use in a meditation room. It is better to have bright colours in a baby's room, as babies tend to respond more readily to them.

The colour of the front door should be in harmony with the direction it faces, for example a door facing north is best painted a shade of blue.

Red bedrooms
Rajasic colours, such as reds, oranges, and shades of terracotta (right above) are ideal for use in bedrooms as they create an atmosphere of warmth, cosiness, and sensuality.

Blue bathrooms
Relaxing, cool shades of blue are perfect for bathrooms (right), where we take the time to relax and soothe the mind and body.

Planning your home

The same principles of Vastu apply, whether you happen to move into a single-storey bungalow or into a multi-storey house. So, when designing the layout of a new house, it is important to keep in mind the most important directions of Vastu (pp.28-9), where the different elements are located (pp.50-3), and the prevalence of the particular gunas (pp.44-7).

While keeping all the components of Vastu in mind, you can then designate the various rooms accordingly, working to your advantage.

Advantage of choice

The advantage of living in a multi-storeyed house is that there are more options open to you when you come to designating the functions of the rooms. For example, the south-east corner of the ground floor is ideal for the kitchen, but the south-east corner of the second floor is ideal for an entirely different purpose, for example, a child's playroom. The south-east corner of the attic would be a good location for the electrical power mains of the house.

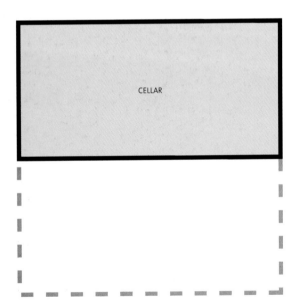

The cellar
If the cellar occupies only part of the area below ground, then it should be located in the northern part of the property.

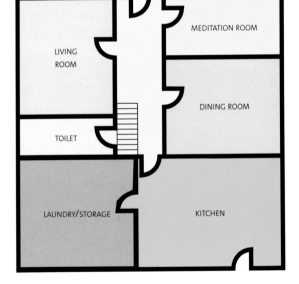

The ground floor
The south-east is ideal for the kitchen, while the other activities should be arranged approximately as shown.

Exterior colour

Yellow or cream symbolize the element of earth and are good colours to choose for the exterior of a house.

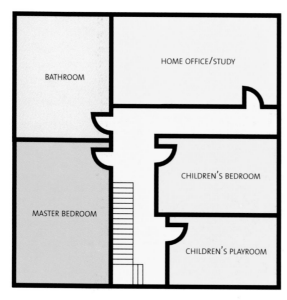

The first floor

The master bedroom should be located in the south-west while children's rooms should be in the east and south-east.

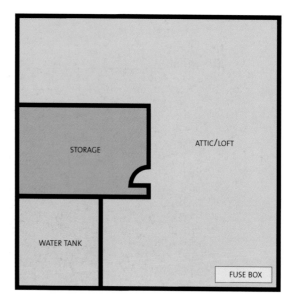

The loft or attic

Storage and heavy tanks should be situated in the south and west, while the fuse box should be in the south-east.

Kitchen: cooking with energy

In India there is a whole science connected with food and health. What we eat, where we eat, and how we eat are all a part of the ancient Indian science of health and vitality called Ayurveda. The written records of this system go back 5,000 years and contain the ancient wisdom of how to establish a balance between the body, mind, and consciousness. The kitchen is associated with health and the nourishment of the family. The correct placement and the arrangement of the kitchen are significant aspects of the Vastu precepts, enhancing the science of Ayurveda.

Kitchen location

For maximum benefit, the kitchen should be located in the south-east section of the home and away from the front door of the house to avoid contaminating energies entering from outside. It must also be well ventilated to prevent cooking smells from permeating the rest of the house. If the house has more than one storey, the kitchen should be situated on the ground floor.

Fire activity

The south-east is the Agni corner, corresponding to the element fire (pp.50-2); because the kitchen houses the cooker and the oven, and is a place of fire activity, the south-east is its natural position. The guna rajas predominates in this area of the house, which is the energy for activity (pp.44-7). An alternative position, also governed by rajas but not as favourable, is the north-west corner. If you are in the process of moving house, check the location of the kitchen before making a final decision. In order to avoid accidents involving fire, ensure that the kitchen is not located in the north-east corner.

Facing east

In Vastu it is said that the food you are preparing will absorb the energy of whichever direction you are facing. Ideally, the cooking hobs should be positioned in such a way that you are facing east when cooking or preparing food. If you face south while cooking, the females of the house may experience problems. Facing south-west will totally disturb the harmony in the household. Facing west is believed to cause skin- or bone-related problems, while facing north while cooking will invite financial losses.

Even if the kitchen is placed in the north-west corner of the house, it is still advisable to face east while cooking. The sink should be in the north-east section of the kitchen, though you should keep a 5 cm (2 in.) gap between the sink and the actual corner (see diagram, facing page). The fridge and the storage cupboards are best arranged along the southern and western walls. If there is a separate oven or microwave oven it should be placed in the south-east section of the room. The washing machine, if it is kept in the kitchen, can be installed on the north-west side.

Directions for the kitchen

This kitchen plan and scheme show equipment and fittings laid out according to the advice of Vastu. The hob faces east, the best direction in which to face while preparing and cooking food, while the sink and draining board are in the north-east corner. The storage units and fridge are positioned along the southern and western walls and the microwave is in the south-east area. The north-west corner is reserved for the washing machine and the eating area fits nicely into the centre.

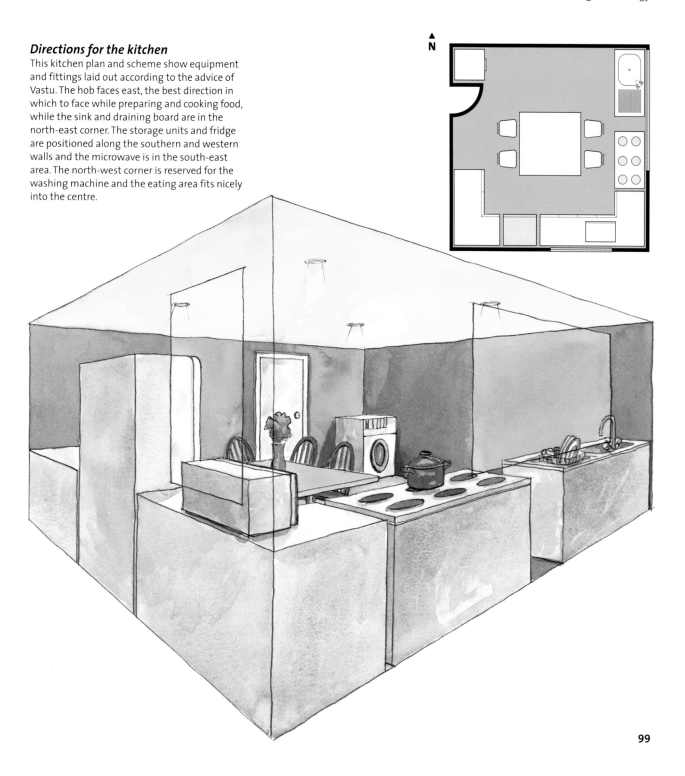

Dining room: eating in harmony

According to Vastu, the dining area is best located in the west. If it is situated in the kitchen itself, then try to organize the seating arrangement in the western section of the room. If the kitchen is located on the north-west side of the house, then the dining area can be placed next to it on the western side. If the kitchen is in the south-east section of the house, the dining area is best positioned in the east. Cooking and eating represent two incompatible energies, so it is preferable to have a separate dining area, or at least a clearly defined section of the kitchen. If you do have a separate dining area, it should not be located too far from the kitchen. It should also be kept well away from both the toilet and the front door.

If possible, the dining table should be rectangular and angled so that you are facing either east or west while eating. Facing east encourages long life, facing west prosperity. It is also perfectly acceptable to face south when eating, but never north.

Creating a calm atmosphere

Ayurveda stresses the importance of sitting quietly at the table and eating with awareness and at a leisurely pace to absorb the greatest nutritional value from food. With the mounting demands of modern life, this is becoming increasingly difficult. For example, eating fast food on the move upsets our delicate internal balance and can create future health problems.

Decorations and colours

The dining area should be decorated in such a way that it is conducive to peaceful eating. There should be soft lighting or candlelight to eat by, away from the influence of the television. The walls can be painted a soft, calming colour, either a light blue or green, and there should not be any loud wallpaper or decorations and furniture that contribute to a heavy, dark atmosphere.

Fruits symbolize abundance, so keeping an image of them in the room invites their presence into the house, and it is a good idea to keep a bowl of fruit on the dining table. Alternatively hang a painting of fruit or another image representing a plentiful harvest on the wall.

Green for calm
A calm atmosphere for enjoying food is created in this minimalist dining room, where a green table setting creates an unusual focus. Pictures on the wall are suitably low key.

Directions for the dining room

This dining room has been arranged according to the principles of Vastu. The rectangular dining table and chairs meet with the requirements that diners should face either west or east and the room has a blue colour scheme to ensure a calm atmosphere. A painting of fruit adorns the north wall to symbolize abundance and plenty.

Living room: sanctuary for relaxation

The living room is the place to sit and relax after a long day or a busy week. It is beneficial if a major part of it occupies the central zone of the building. According to Vastu, this central portion is not conducive to major activities as it receives the least amount of cosmic energy, and so is the best place for rest and relaxation. In India, houses are often built around an open central courtyard, where the inhabitants can sit in the cool evenings.

The living room can be located in any direction, as long as part of it occupies the centre of the house. However, Vastu practitioners often recommend the west or north. The west is a highly auspicious direction, naturally helping to promote memory and intelligence. The west is also the exalted position for Mercury, the planet of communication and social activities, so is a good place for entertaining. The northern direction is better for a sitting room-cum-library, as it is influenced by Jupiter, the planet of learning and study.

Seating arrangements

The most important items in the sitting room are the sofa and chairs. As they are heavy, they are best placed in the south or west. This also ensures that when seated you will be facing either east or north. The northern direction is known as *Kubera Sthana* and bestows wealth and power on those who face north. However, it is important that doors or windows are not directly behind the sofa, as you will not feel fully relaxed while seated.

Other heavy furniture, such as bookshelves, should be along the south or west walls, while objects connected with fire or heat, radiators or electrical items, are best positioned towards the south-east. The telephone can be in either the south-east or the north-west. Although it is electrical, the north-west is connected to air, which governs communication. Family photographs should be in the south-west corner.

The walls of the living room can be painted calming blue or green. Alternatively, if the room is more of a social venue, yellow is a good choice, as it is mentally stimulating. Be aware of your choice of pictures, as they can profoundly affect the atmosphere (pp.120-1).

Colour and texture combinations
The combination of warm colours, rich textures, with light, fresh paintwork create a relaxing living area in this converted warehouse.

Your living room

As advised by Vastu, the heaviest items of furniture are placed in the west and south, so that those seated are facing either north or east and the door and window are not directly behind the sofa. The bookcase is kept along the west wall and the television and radiator are located along the east wall. The telephone is situated in the north-west and pictures of the ancestors are in the south-west corner. Calming blue-green or yellow walls are suitable choices for this room.

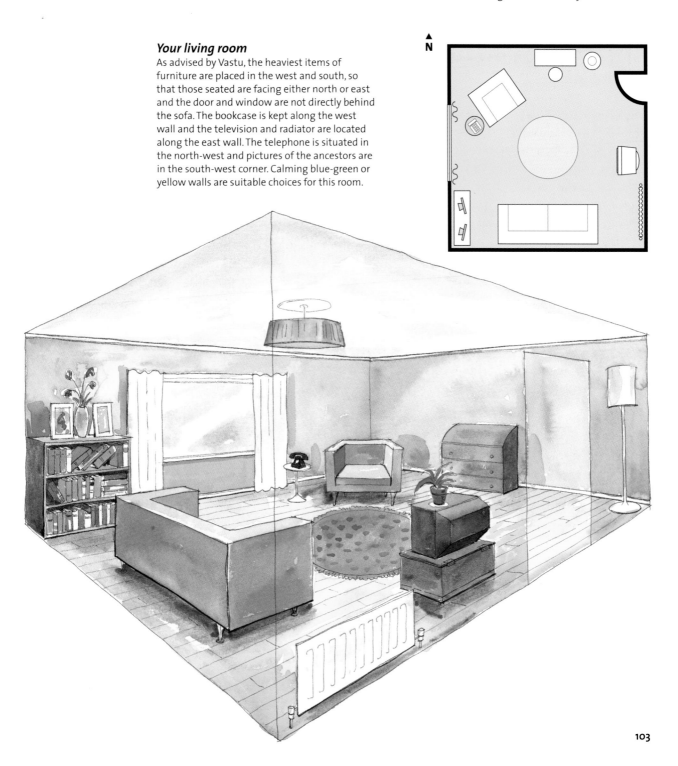

Lighting: bringing life to your home

Light is a very important element within the home and good lighting is naturally uplifting. Light, called *jyotis* in India, corresponds to the principle of sight, and is represented by the sattva guna, the energy of clear perceptions and pure knowledge (pp.44-7). Joy is the inherent sattva attribute that gives both pleasure and illumination. The sattva corner of a property is the north-east, which represents creative, positive energy as opposed to the heat and fire of the south-east. For this reason it is preferable to have natural light entering from the north-east side of the property.

The light emanating from the sun feeds the earth and gives both food and joy to all life. Natural light provides the most balanced source of energy, so it is favourable if your home and workplace have access to an abundant supply of

natural light. It is always preferable to have too much natural light than too little, although blinds and curtains can be used to control the flow of sunlight into a room. Because they are soft and fluid, curtains encourage a softer atmosphere in a room, whereas blinds are hard-edged and create a more systematic ambience. Blinds with horizontal slats allow prana to enter, whereas vertical slats block the flow.

Light is very easy to manipulate and can quickly alter the atmosphere of a room. If the lighting in a room is either evenly distributed or overhead, then the room is considered neutral. More light fittings positioned along the north and east walls are positive, as light emanating from the north-east represents approaching prosperity. However, if the main source of lighting in a room is from the south-east corner, then this is considered negative.

The Ancients considered light to be the eye of God, so all lamps were made from the best materials—either ceramic, metal, or a good-quality wood—and were beautifully adorned and decorated. Decorative lighting also enhances an atmosphere more effectively than stark fluorescent strips.

Artificial lighting

If you have dark rooms or corridors in your house, these areas will require good interior lighting to bring them back to life. In such environments it is important to install full-spectrum bulbs, which are composed of all the colours of the rainbow. Bulbs that shine with only a portion of the spectrum can cause restlessness and unease. Candlelight and natural fire light are both naturally soothing and can be used to create a relaxing atmosphere. Different-coloured bulbs or lampshades can also be used to change the mood of a room.

Candlelight
The light of candles (below) is naturally soothing and can be used to create a relaxing atmosphere.

Natural sunlight
Large windows on two sides (left) admit plenty of natural light, to enhance the relaxing atmosphere of this room.

Bedrooms

In Hindu mythology, night was a time to forget, to let go of daily cares. In Vedic philosophy, it is said that deep sleep is when we reunite with the source. This union is blissful and fills us with the joy of pure existence, peace, and happiness. If we sleep deeply, we awaken refreshed, ready for the new day. Quality of sleep is far more important than length of time; deep, uninterrupted sleep is essential for well being.

A place of refuge

Vastu emphasizes the importance of creating an environment for us to feel secure and relaxed enough to sleep soundly. The bedroom is the place of refuge, where we are unprotected, no longer alert to possible danger. The Ancient Rishis discovered that certain locations are more conducive to peaceful sleep than others. Vastu identifies these areas in the context of the master, children's, and guest rooms, and recommends the best position and room plan for each.

The direction in which you sleep is important. The Rishis discovered a correlation between the magnetic field of the earth and the human body, which acts like a magnetic pole, with the head corresponding to the North Pole. If the head is towards the north when sleeping, the two poles repel each other. This affects blood circulation and disturbs sleep, and may even cause long-term chronic health problems. For this reason, the Shaastras advise sleeping with your head towards the east or the south, never the north.

Master bedroom

The master bedroom should be one of the largest rooms in the house and inhabited by the principal adults of the house. The best location is in the south-west. This direction receives the least light, and is therefore suitable for a bedroom. The south-west quarter of the house is associated with the element earth. Earth is the most stable element, being both inert and inactive, so it provides the most peaceful and restful conditions for sleep. The south-west corner is also where the energy of tamas lies, the guna that induces a natural inclination towards inactivity and sleep.

Choosing a position

If you cannot allocate a south-west room for the master bedroom, then a room on either the west or the south side of the house should be chosen. Both will benefit from the influence of the element earth and the tamasic energy of the south-west. If you live in a one-room apartment or studio, try to organize the space so that the sleeping area is in the south-west corner of the room. If your house has more than one floor, bedrooms should be on the first floor, or higher, but never at ground level, otherwise you will feel exposed and your sleep will be disturbed.

Once you have decided on the location of the master bedroom, it is important to consider its design. The most important feature is the bed; indeed, ancient Vastu texts contain descriptions of the exact proportions and design of the bed. If possible, it should be made of a good-quality wood, wood being benign and warm; metal is not recommended, as it is associated with Saturn and can be cold and oppressive.

The ancient texts say that the legs of the bed should not exceed one span, which is the equivalent of 40 cm (16 in.). The width of the bed should be approximately 1.3 m (4 ft.), about the width of a queen-size mattress, and 2 m (7 ft.) long. There should be a headboard, which should be carved with flower or leaf motifs. The bed needs to be an exquisite place, with fresh, clean sheets, and adorned in an appropriate manner, so that you can indulge in its pleasures and rest contented. It is a good idea to keep lavender by the bed or to burn lavender oil, as it helps to relax the mind. The bed, being the heaviest item in the room, should be kept in the south-west corner. Any other heavy furniture should be located on either the south or the west side of the bedroom. Keep the dressing table, along with any jewellery boxes, against the north wall. Mirrors should be kept on the north or east walls only.

Lighting

Avoid having bright lights in the room, because they have a stimulating effect and can disturb you. If you have candles in the room, then try to keep them in the south-east corner to avoid any accidents involving fire. Paint the walls with soft, light tones at the red end of the colour spectrum. Red is a good colour to enhance feelings of warmth, love, and romance (pp.94-5).

Directions for the master bedroom

To arrange the master bedroom according to Vastu principles, position the bed in the west and the heavy wardrobe and furniture in the south-west. The north wall is the best choice for keeping the dressing table and any valuables, such as jewellery. The pink colour scheme is appropriate for this bedroom, enhancing the feeling of warmth and cosiness.

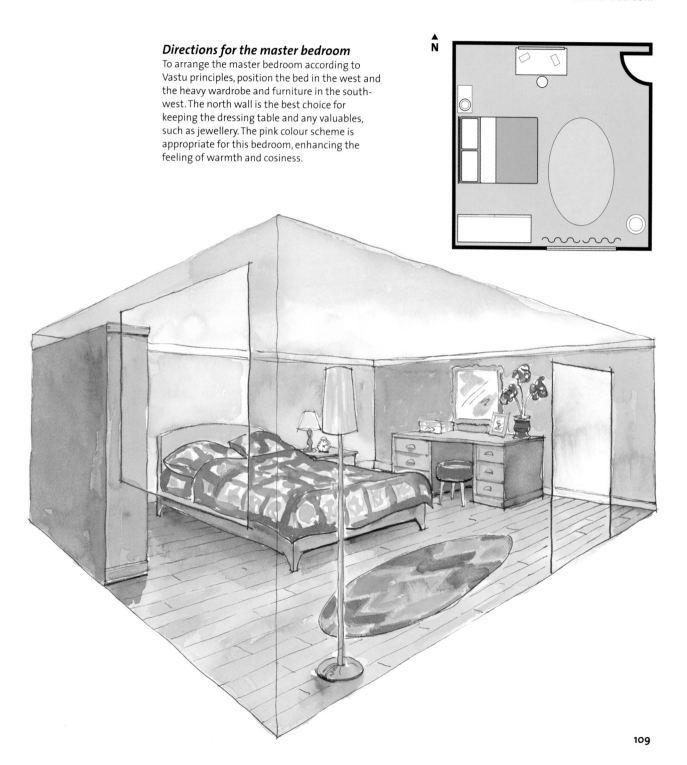

Bedroom for children

Children have different energy from adults because they embody new life and vitality. The best location for a child's bedroom is on the east side of the house, as young children are often put to bed in the early evening, when the sun is in the western hemisphere and it is still daylight. For this reason, you may want to install heavy blackout curtains or blinds that block out daylight very effectively to encourage the right atmosphere for sleep.

Sattva for children

The east side of the house is influenced by the energy of sattva, which supports new life and growth (pp.44-7), so it is ideal for children. If the layout of your house does not allow this, then the north-west is also suitable, especially for daughters. Both of these directions are influenced by the active energy of rajas, which is appropriate for children, who may spend some time each day playing in their bedrooms.

Key directions

A child's bed should also be pleasantly decorated and positioned somewhere along the south or west wall. While reading, doing projects, or other creative activities children should sit facing the east, as this will enhance their mental capacity. They can also face north, but should avoid the west and never be allowed to face south at all. The desk or table should be kept away from the north-east corner by leaving a small gap.

If possible, it is best not to install a computer or television in a child's bedroom. Apart from the fact that children are better off playing creatively, keeping electrical equipment in a bedroom has a detrimental effect on the room's atmosphere and could prevent children getting good-quality sleep.

Colours

Beware of using an excess of clashing colours and conflicting images in the child's room, as research has shown that children can suffer from over-stimulation, whereby they are unable to concentrate for extended periods. However, the door can be painted with primary colours.

The organized child
The room should be decorated in a way that is appealing to the child and be furnished so that s/he can keep it organized.

Directions for a child's room

According to Vastu, the child's desk should be kept away from the north-east corner by leaving a small gap between it and the north wall and the child should face east while engaged in activities requiring concentration and thinking. The bed should be located along the south or west walls while cupboards and bookshelves can be placed along north and west walls. The centre of the room is best kept clear so that there is a good-sized play area available.

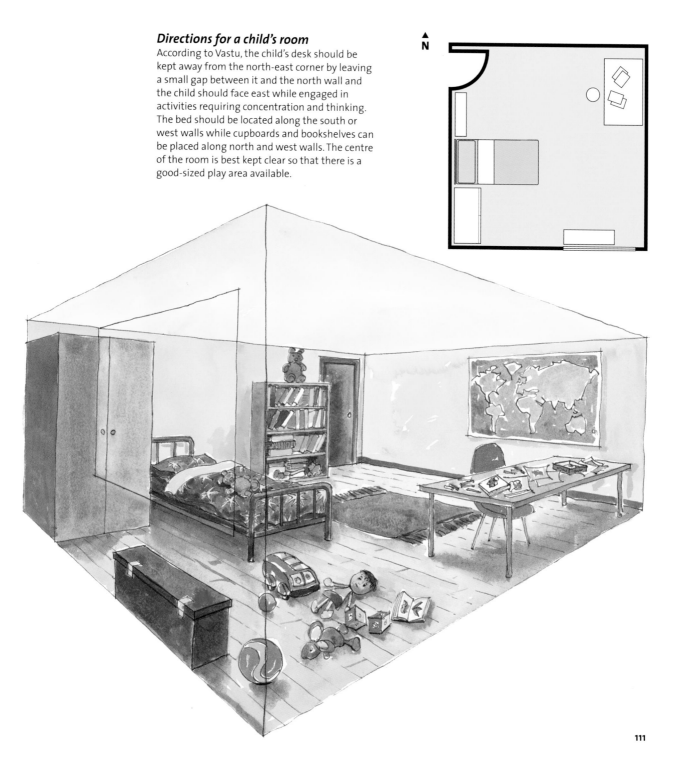

Guest room

In general, all bedrooms should be located on solid ground so a spare bedroom over a garage is not advisable—the movement of a car driving in and out creates restless energy. Equally, a spare bedroom should not be positioned over a verandah or basements, as they can cause mental instability. The guest room door should not be in direct alignment with the master bedroom door, as it can cause conflict between the two occupants. If you have the space in your home for a guest

room, then it is best located in the north-west or west. The north-west quadrant is ruled by the element water and the energy of rajas, causing both restlessness and instability. Since guests come and go, perhaps staying for variable lengths of time, this area provides a perfect platform for transitory events.

Positioning

Keep all heavy furniture along the south and west walls. The visitor's head can be positioned towards the west while sleeping, as it is not a long-term situation, though the east and south directions are more favourable. Good ventilation is important, although it is better to have fewer windows in the room, for this will enhance your guest's feeling of protection and ensure greater darkness for a better sleep.

If there is excessive interference from street lights outside the windows, then hang thick curtains so that the room remains dark. Position the bed away from the door and windows to ensure thorough protection from draughts, which can cause a cricked neck as well as numerous other ailments.

It is not a good idea to keep a television, computer, or an excess of electrical equipment in the guest room, or, indeed, in any bedroom, for they charge the atmosphere and prevent proper sleep. Many people use a guest room as a study when it is not in use, so cover up computers if you cannot move them out.

Pictures and colours

Try to avoid hanging pictures or mirrors directly over the bed, for they can cause low-level anxiety. The walls can be a neutral colour such as green or blue; alternatively, try something brighter and more joyful such as yellow or orange, though you should avoid white (see pp.94-5). If the room remains unoccupied for some time between guests, then periodically place fresh flowers in it and open the windows to keep the room aired.

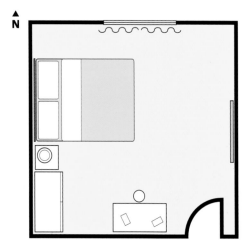

Plan for the guest room
In accordance with Vastu (above) the bed is along the west wall, and away from the door, and the room is painted an uplifting shade of yellow.

Warm and welcoming
An inviting guest room (left) should be cosy, airy, decorated neutrally, but with some uplifting shades as accent points.

Bathroom: cleanse & rejuvenate

Traditionally, in a typical dwelling in India, the bathroom and toilet were outside, away from the house. Only stately buildings or royal palaces had inside bathrooms, and here the bathroom or toilet was located in the south-west of the building, or genital area of Vastu Purusha, located on the squares of Vibhuda, Indraha, Mrigaha, or Douvarikaha (p.60). The south-west is also the best location for the master bedroom, which is convenient at night. *En suite* bathrooms are not generally recommended since the bedroom and the bathroom have different functions. It is therefore preferable to have two separate rooms with separate entrances to ensure that the energy of neither room is disturbed. In addition to the south-west, the north-west is also a good location for a bathroom, this being the water area of the house. The east is also an acceptable location for a bathroom without a toilet.

The importance of the moon

The bathroom is ruled by the moon and is a place for cleansing and rejuvenation. As written in the *Mayamata*, an ancient text that refers to Vastu, the bathroom should be rendered beautiful, free from dirt and hair, and filled with flowers, plants, and fragrant substances. It advises putting on clean, white silk robes after bathing. Similar to the moon in character, the bathroom requires reflective surfaces, such as mirrors, placed along north and east walls only. The toilet should not be too close to the kitchen. According to Vastu it should be installed so that it is aligned along the north-south line; when sitting you should face north. In a larger bathroom it is better if the toilet is away from windows or doors for privacy. In India squat toilets are common, squatting being the natural position. To help, place a stool in front of the toilet to raise the feet.

Bathroom colour and light
Paint the bathroom a light, refreshing colour, such as off-white, light blue, or green. There should be subdued lighting—bathing by candlelight is recommended as being particularly relaxing.

Bathroom layout

Following the advice of Vastu, the toilet is placed against the south wall and away from the window. The bath, which is the heaviest object, i s in the south-west corner. The bathroom is associated with the moon, and is a good place for reflective surfaces such as glass and tiles. Mirrors should be kept along the north and east walls.

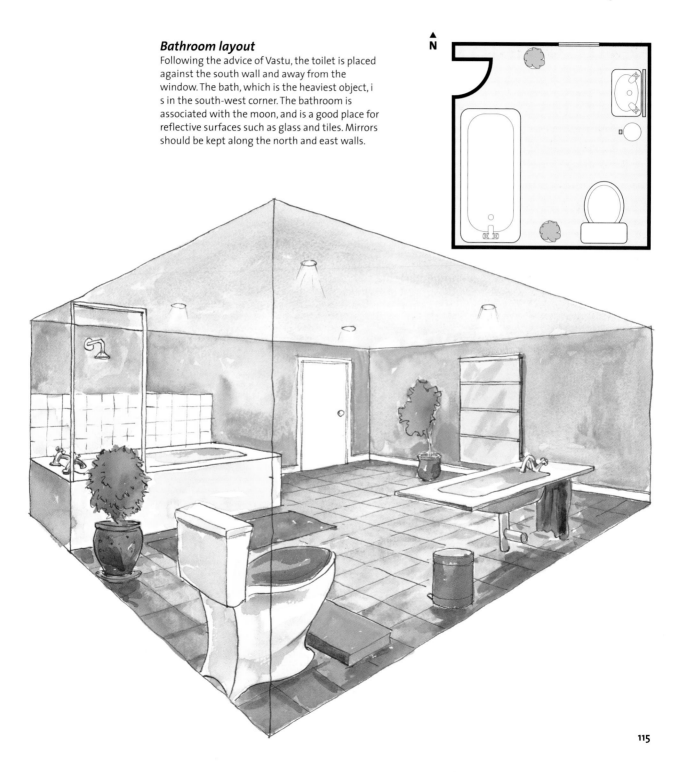

One-room living: lofts & studios

Even if you live in one room, in a loft space, or studio, separate areas can be divided in a similar manner to houses and apartments with multiple rooms. Using screens is also a convenient way of separating different functions. It is better if the studio is located either on the first floor or higher. Basements tend to be dark and damp.

Creating more space

Storage space is often the greatest challenge of living in a single room. Storage units and other heavy furniture such as beds and wardrobes need to be kept along the south and west walls. It is a good idea in small spaces to have a bed that converts into a settee or to have a table that folds away, so that the room can be used for different functions. Another idea to relieve the monotony of living in a single room is to raise the floor level in the south or west, which has the added advantage of blocking the south-west corner, making it heavier and higher, thereby conforming to Vastu principles. This prevents negative influences from entering the room. Another alternative, to create more floor space, is to have a loft-style bed, or mezzanine. Again, this should be located along the south or west walls only.

The kitchen

The kitchen area needs to be situated either in the south-east corner of the room or the north-west, while the cooker should be installed so that you face east when preparing food (see also pp.98-9).

The bathroom should be situated in the east, south-west, or north-west. Avoid studios with the bathroom in the north-east, as it will drain your finances. The north-east corner of the space should have no heavy furniture and be kept as open as possible. Do not put heavy furniture in the centre of the room.

Working from home

If you work from home, then the desk should face either east or north. The television or computer can be placed towards the south-east of the room, or the fire corner. It is soothing to have natural elements such as plants or a small fountain in the north-east of the room. It is always more of a challenge to keep a small space clean and organized, but it is important that you do, to prevent stagnant energies accumulating.

Clutter

Just as the entry of positive energy into a home is important, so too is its circulation. Clutter can be one of the biggest obstacles to a harmonious environment and the problem is often accentuated in one-room living. "Clutter" is objects that look disorganized, or too many possessions crammed into a small space. One of the greatest challenges to one-room living is restricting the amount of furniture and shelving units to a bare minimum. An apartment with separate rooms can absorb an array of furniture, while a single room cannot. A cluttered

environment reflects a cluttered mind and is a manifestation of postponed decisions. The vital decision of whether to throw an object away or keep it is never actually made. In one-room living it is necessary to become ruthless and throw out anything that you are not sure about. Such objects often have bad energies and by doing this you are subconsciously making way for new, positive energy to enter your life. If you are having difficulty letting go of excess possessions, then temporarily rent a small storage space away from your home.

Prana flows in meandering paths, so keeping open spaces for this energy to circulate is very

beneficial and will increase your personal happiness and health. Clutter focused on a particular area of a room will affect the corresponding area of your life. For example, clutter in the northern section will obstruct the flow of prosperity into your life. For this reason keep a watchful eye on the tops of work surfaces, tables, fridge tops, and counters to check for the accumulation of objects which are not actually being used at present.

Housework can be tiresome, but it is vital to keep a small home clean and tidy and you will feel refreshed and energized once the job is accomplished; this simple wisdom of purification is the key to enhancing the energy of a space.

Studio layout

The plan (above) shows a possible layout for a studio or loft apartment. The bedroom is in the south-west and the kitchen is in the south-east, with an open centre, complying with Vastu recommendations.

Downtown Manhattan

This city street (left) is filled with large loft apartments that were once all industrial units.

Loft apartment

A mezzanine floor (previous page) has been added to this loft apartment to add extra space. Ideally the floor should be raised in either the south or the west of the room to enhance the Vastu of the space.

What's on the wall?

Pictures and paintings can have a profound effect on the atmospheres of the home and working environments, as they evoke what is called *rasa* in Indian philosophy. Rasa is a strong sentiment or aesthetic experience that gives rise to *bhava*, meaning a particular mental state or mood. As described by René Daulmal in his book *Rasa*, bhava is "a moment of consciousness provoked by the medium of art and coloured by a particular pathos". The mental perceptions and feelings we have are said to be the reins that govern our physical lives. Altogether there are nine rasa, which cover the whole spectrum of human emotions, ranging from fear to excitability (see box, below left).

The rasa that are deemed highly suitable for interiors are known as *shingara, hasya,* and *sahanta*, the seductive, the comic, and the peaceful. So a combination of images that are evocative of these three emotions are recommended for use in the home.

On the wall

Certain interiors cause particular rasa, or emotions. There are nine of these.

1 **Shingara** is seductive, induced by beauty, ornamentation, and pleasing forms.
2 **Hasya** is comic and excitable.
3 **Karuna** is pathetic; it gives rise to the feelings of separation, sorrow, and abandonment, and is associated with the colour grey.
4 **Roudra** is the furious emotion, bringing anger and harshness.
5 **Vira** is heroic, bestowing feelings of nobility and prowess.
6 **Bhayanaka** is fearful, associated with the colour black.
7 **Adbhuta** is the feeling of amazement and is awe-inspiring.
8 **Bibhatsa** is the feeling of repulsion.
9 **Sahanta** is peaceful and meditative.

Picture positions

Where pictures are hung also needs to be considered carefully: images such as fruit, flowers, and blossoming trees symbolize vitality and are best hung on east or north walls. Pictures denoting wealth and abundance, such as Lakshmi, the goddess of plenty, or gemstones and jewels, should be hung on the north wall. Landscapes depicting mountains should be hung on the south and west walls only, for if they are hung on the north wall they will obstruct the flow of prosperity. Landscapes containing water, such as pictures of lakes and rivers, should be kept on the north and east walls.

Animal images

Images of carnivorous animals indicate a ruthless and greedy attitude towards life and should therefore be avoided. The eagle, in particular, represents the most extreme of selfish natures

and a blood-sucking temperament. Those animal pictures that are good to hang on the walls include horses, which are a representation of strength, expansion, and virility, cows, which are symbols of peace and abundance, and elephants, which suggest strength and slow, steady success.

Other unsuitable images for use in the home are those that depict bloody battle scenes or that feature guns and weaponry, barren landscapes, or pictures with bare, thorny trees, and any pictures that are dark and gloomy in colour, atmosphere, or content.

Suitable rasas

Shingara, hasya, and sahanta are the three rasas that are the most suitable subjects for the home.

Shingara

Sandro Botticelli's *The Birth of Venus* (above right) is a typical example of shingara, being seductive in content, beautiful, and pleasing in form.

Sahanta

This peaceful and meditative landscape (Auguste Renoir's *La Seine à Champrosay,* right) is a perfect example of sahanta.

What's on top & down below?

The roof of a building is a significant aspect of Vastu to consider. Important features include its shape, the way in which it slopes, and whether it is supporting any heavy weights. All these details subtly act upon the psyche of the inhabitants.

A sloping roof should be even on both sides or, if it is irregular, slope more towards the north or the east and less towards the south or west. If there are chimney stacks on the roof, they should be on the south or the west side only.

Heavy loads

In New York City many of the apartment buildings have overhead water storage tanks that are very heavy. These should always be on the south or west of the building and never on the north-east corner, as the north-eastern section of the roof cannot tolerate heavy burdens. Any weight located there will obstruct the flow of prosperity, and the inhabitants will not be able to advance. If the apartment has a roof terrace, it is better if it extends towards the north or the east of the building.

Aerials and dishes

For the best reception, you should connect your outside television aerial or satellite dish at the south-east section of the building, the fire corner. Any telephone lines or outside lights are also best kept on the south-east side of the property.

The flat roof
Houses with flat roofs are considered neutral, that is as long as there are no overhead water storage tanks located in the wrong place.

A roof with two sloping faces
This style of roof is considered to be auspicious if it slopes towards the north or the east. Avoid buildings that have a pent roof sloping in the opposite direction.

If possible attach the drainage system on the roof so that the water can flow from the south and west and can run off the north or the east side of the building.

Skylights and tiles

If your home has any skylight windows or if you are planning to install some, then they should be located on the north or the east sides of the roof. The roof tiles need to be well maintained and aligned, and cracked and broken ones replaced. Ideally tiles should be made of good quality materials such as slate.

A pyramid-shaped roof
This roof is neutral as it slopes evenly on all sides. Ideally the chimney stack should be located on the south or west sides.

Down below

Underground spaces affect the energy of the building you live in, whether it is a house with a small cellar or an apartment building with a sizeable underground car park. In looking at the lie of the land, the main principle to observe is that the land should be even or slope from the south or west towards the north or east. The same paradigm applies to underground spaces. A cellar on the south or west side would reverse the principle and cause many problems for the owners.

Cellars

The cellar should be located either on the north or on the east side of the property, but never just in the south-west corner. It is preferable if the entire floor consists of a single basement. The stairs leading down into the basement should also slope from the south or west towards the north or east. Heavy items of furniture that are stored in the basement are best kept along the south and west walls. However, if there is a generator or boiler kept in the cellar, it can be placed in the south-east corner.

Car parks

If there is an underground car park forming part of the apartment block, this will create a restless energy in the rest of the building. If this is unavoidable the north-east corner of the car park should be left empty.

Basement apartments

It is best to avoid living in basement apartments or locating your office in a basement. Living below ground level can cause mental instability, as you will tend to feel more vulnerable. In general, basements have less access to natural light and cross ventilation compared with apartments situated above ground.

Garden sanctuary

Many thousands of years ago the Ancient Sages lived among trees in forests. They grasped the deep connection between humankind and nature. The same is true of our ancestors in the West, the English word paradise being a transliteration of the Persian word *pairidaeza*, referring to a walled garden. A similar idea persists in the Indian psyche: an ancient Indian text connected to Vastu, the *Brhat Samhita*, declares that "the gods always play where groves are near rivers, mountains and ponds and in towns with pleasure gardens". Brindavan, the garden of the most popular deity Lord Krishna, an incarnation of Vishnu, is seen as the land of eternal love, and is said to be filled with enchanted deer, flocks of peacocks, and groves of trees. The landscape in India is filled with sacred sites; these places of power have strong connections with the macrocosm and the microcosm.

With this in mind it is easy to understand why the garden is such a sanctuary: it is here that we can commune with nature and observe the cycle of the seasons, even in the midst of a bustling city. If you live in a high-rise apartment in the centre of a city or in a place that has no garden, it is especially important to remain connected to the natural world. Cultivate an array of window boxes or potted plants, or take long walks in a nearby park to immerse yourself in the sights and smells of nature. The colour green is particularly important for our well being; indeed, in colour therapy, green is used for re-balancing.

Planning your garden

If your property has a garden or if you are looking for a home with a garden, then there are a few aspects to consider. Firstly you need to investigate the size and the shape of the garden, and secondly its position in relation to the house.

Vastu recommends that the garden is either square or rectangular, though it is best to avoid a long, narrow rectangle. You should reject any irregular-shaped sites, especially if the north-east corner is cut off. Conversely it is considered a prime site if the north-east corner is extended. If your garden is a negative, irregular shape then it is worth landscaping it to square the corners.

Imaginary lines

To determine how the garden lies in relation to the house you need to measure the invisible lines lying between the corners of the building and the garden. For example, the north-east line is the imaginary line connecting the north-east corner

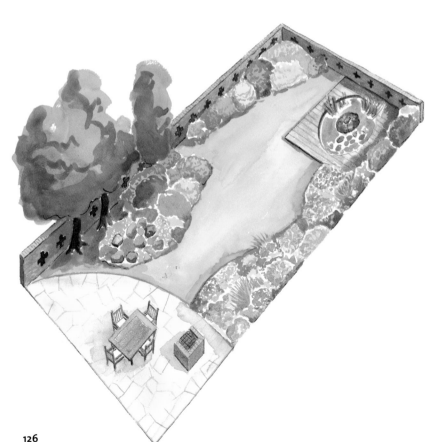

Your garden
This garden has been designed according to Vastu principles. The tall trees are in the south-west corner, offering protection from the sun's infra-red rays. There is a pond with a small fountain in the north-east corner, bringing increased prana and prosperity. The barbecue area is located in the south-east section, in the Agni, or fire, corner. The garden is enclosed and protected to allow for the movement of prana.

of the building to the north-east corner of the garden. According to Vastu, the north-east line should always be the longest and the south-east line the shortest for perfect harmony to prevail.

Testing the soil

Before choosing a home with a garden it is a good idea to check the soil and observe what vegetation is already growing. The soil should be pleasing to the eye and mind, compact, and smooth. It can be a reddish colour, yellow, or blackish, and should hold water. It should also be free from pebbles, ants, bones, sludge, holes, rats, and

stumps. The Ancient Sages used to taste the soil to make sure that it was not too acidic or alkaline.

Make sure that there are no thorny shrubs, as these will keep prosperity from the house. Avoid a property with large trees very close to the house, especially if they are taller than it. Large trees and bushes are best situated on the south-west side, as they will supply a pure source of oxygen and also provide protection from the infra-red rays of the afternoon sun. Small plants and green lawns should be on the north-east side, offering a clear passage for the morning sun.

Past associations

It is the custom in India, when moving to a new property, to till the soil to remove past associations, along with any bad spirits that may be lurking. This also gives new life and air to the soil and represents a fresh new beginning. It is also customary to sow some grain, which is then cut and offered to the departed spirit.

When landscaping a garden, try to incorporate the element water: the Ancient Sages revered water, for it is written in the *Upanishads* that water transforms into prana. If you build a pond, it should never be positioned in the south-west

Lifeblood

Water represents the lifeblood of the garden, especially if it is flowing freely, since the silvery sound of running water, together with the play of light bouncing from it, are both deeply soothing. If the water is running along a channel, then it is best if it flows from the south towards the north or from the west towards the east.

Caring for the garden
It is good to grow an abundance of bright, colourful flowers, especially in the north section, to attract wealth. Plants are living entities that greatly enhance prana, though they must be well maintained. It is important to remove dead or dying plants as they will affect that aspect of your life; a dying plant in the south-east will affect the health of the women living in the house.

corner. Any depression acts as a receiving zone, and a pond is a depression, so for maximum benefit, place it in the north-east section. However, make sure that it is not crossing the north-east line. A pond should be filled with large golden fish for enhanced prosperity and water lilies, the symbol of the universe, should be grown on its surface.

Trees and flowers

Trees should be planted on the south and west borders of the garden, but not too closely together, otherwise they will choke one another. Flowering fruit trees are good to have, for they represent fertility, renewal, and abundance. The garden should be filled with fragrant flowers, as pleasant aromas help lift the spirit. Heavy stone figures or rock gardens should be placed in the south-west corner, along with other heavy items such as the compost heap. If you have a barbecue, build it towards the south-east, or fire, corner.

The shed

Carefully balancing all the elements within the boundaries of a property is the skill of the Vastu practitioner. The most important aspect to consider is that prana is entering and flowing freely in the garden. External structures positioned in the wrong place can restrict the flow of prana, and the lifeblood of the environment is lost. A shed in your garden may appear harmless, but if it is badly positioned it could disrupt well being and harmony.

The south-west corner of the garden is the prime position for the shed, which should also touch the fences. This position will ensure that all the positively charged energy does not escape, and will prevent negative forces from entering.

If the garden extends to the north or east of the house, then the shed should be closer to the main building. Leave as much space as possible between the shed and the outside wall. If the shed is near the north-east corner, be careful that it does not cross the north-east line, an imaginary line connecting the north-east corner of the house to the north-east corner of the garden. If the shed crosses this line, it will obstruct the natural flow of energy and cause financial problems.

A building in the south-east corner should also be closer to the house, leaving more room between it and the outside wall. However, if there is already a building in the south-east corner, it should be removed or another building constructed in the south-west to block this corner as well. If there is a structure in the north-west corner, it should be removed. Failing this, all three corners (south-west, south-east, and north-west), should be blocked.

Placing your shed
A badly positioned garden shed can restrict the flow of prana into the property, disrupting the natural harmony of the environment.

Key
- ■ The garden and its border
- ■ The house
- ■ If there is a shed in the north-west corner, it should either be removed to the south-west, and the south-east corner should also be blocked.
- ■ If the shed is located in the north-east corner, then it should be placed closer to the house, but without crossing the north-east line.
- ■ The north-east line.
- ■ The south-west corner is the prime position for the shed.

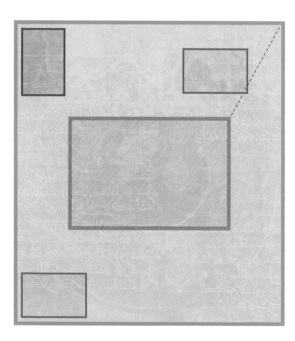

▲
N

Walls & fences to energize your home

Vastu Purusha is depicted as a demon confined within a square. The square represents the limitations or boundaries in which the energies of the universe, symbolized by Vastu Purusha, are operating. The boundary walls to any site or garden are very important according to the Vastu precepts: not only do they define the parameters of a property but they also control the flow of energy in and out of your home. The work of a Vastu practitioner is confined to the harmonious adjustment of all the elements within the boundary walls. Traditionally these were erected before construction started on a new building to prevent any negative influences entering from the neighbouring property. For instance, if the neighbour's pond happens to be in the south-west corner of your property, it could have disastrous consequences for you. It is therefore essential to keep your garden fences well maintained.

Ideal proportions

Ideally the shape of your property should be either a square or a rectangle, with all the corners at right angles. The north-east corner especially should never be cut across or rounded, but at a 90° angle or less, never more. The perfect measurement for correct proportion, or *maana,* as it is called in Vastu, is for the height of the outer walls to be three-quarters the height of the front door. The walls along the south and west sides should be 30 cm (12 in.) higher than the north and east walls. However, it is recommended that the south and west walls are thicker and slightly higher than the north and east walls. This is to keep positive energy gathered within the confines of the property and to stop negative energy entering from the south-west. Fences that have vertically spaced sections of either wood or iron, such as iron railings (see facing page), obstruct prana more effectively than those that are horizontally spaced, like the ones often used

N

WATER FEATURE

SHED

HOUSE

South-west wall
Do not worry if the south-west wall extends directly from the house (left): it will not cause any problems.

for paddocks. For this reason it is better to have open horizontal fencing along the north-east side of the property. If you construct a wall on the north and east sides of the property, then ensure there are spaced vents or openings along it to allow energy to flow freely.

A brick wall acts as a barrier to all types of forces and is particularly required to keep out negative ones. Brick walls are especially for the south and west boundaries of the property, both to keep out negative forces and to harbour positive prana. Under certain circumstances, a wall without vents may be required in the north or the east of the property to keep out negative influences, for instance, if there is a vedhi shola such as a road pointing directly at the house. If the gradient of the land naturally slopes from north to south or west to east, then building a brick wall without vents is also advisable.

Types of fence

Classic iron railings (above left), commonly seen outside city terraced houses, block prana more than horizontal slats (above), which are often used to fence in horses. So it is preferable to used the latter along the north-east side of the property. If there is a brick wall along the north and east sides, then it is a good idea to leave openings or vents at intervals along it (see left) to allow free energy flow.

Living in a city

In ancient times entire Indian cities, such as the holy city of Dwarka in Gujarat, were built in keeping with Vastu principles, to ensure the success and well being of all the inhabitants. According to legend, Krishna, the most popular god of the Hindu pantheon, ruled from the city of Dwarka in his adult life. Unfortunately modern cities are not as well planned: often they have been built and added to again and again over long periods to become a chaotic mass of conflicting energies. So if you live in a city it is doubly important to design your living and working spaces carefully, so that they will deflect harmful influences.

Ideally, Vastu advises the avoidance of a home with common walls, as this inhibits the natural flow of light and air. We have seen in the last hundred years how living closely together creates congestion and has increased the number of asthma sufferers in cities. Unfortunately, because of high land costs and ever-growing populations, living in apartment blocks in compacted spaces has become the norm. To combat the effects of asthma and other respiratory-related problems, it is essential that you admit as much fresh air into your home as possible. Use fans to circulate the air and keep house plants to absorb pollutants. Dust quickly builds up in the city, so keeping the apartment clean and dust-free is also an important part of improving air quality. Try to install a small indoor fountain to purify and freshen the air.

Let as much light as possible into the apartment by keeping the windows clean and pruning large trees that might block the flow of light. If the apartment is dark, then install good interior lighting and spend some time each day outside, walking during lunch breaks, walking to the bus or subway, or carrying out errands.

Noise and heat

Other environmental problems connected to living in the city are noise and heat. We are bombarded by so many abrasive sounds that in some cases this results in long-term hearing defects. It is always better to look for living spaces on quieter back streets and away from the main hubbub. If you live on a busy road or junction, try hanging thick curtains or double-glaze the windows to create a buffer zone between the interior calm and the noise outside.

Living in densely populated cities also creates what are known as heat islands, meaning that the temperature in the city is a few degrees higher than outside. During heat waves temperatures can be challenging, especially for older residents or anyone with a heart condition. Again fans, plants, and fountains help to cool the apartment. It is also imperative in large cities to have as many green spaces as possible, as these have a substantial impact on the environment: not only do they help to remove toxins from the air but they also cool the city and absorb noise. Without them life in the city would become unbearable.

Misalignment

Many towns and cities have been built with no knowledge of Vastu or proper orientation. Unless you live in a city like New York, where the roads are built on a grid system and orientated to the cardinal points, it is unlikely that your home will be perfectly aligned. However, all is not lost: certain measures can be taken to rectify a mis-aligned building, although you should really employ a Vastu practitioner to assess your individual needs, as the necessary alterations will usually be complicated and technical.

A building has to be between 12° and 30° out of alignment to be what is termed a "tilted" site. If the building is tilted at 30°, then the major cardinal directions become the corner points and the junctional directions are found along the centre of the building (see p.41). This situation is fine as long as all the rooms of the house are properly located.

When a building is tilted between 12° and 30°, then two of the angles grow—this is known as angular growth—and become positive, while the other two diminish and become negative (see below). In this situation it is important to strengthen the two corners that have become weaker by providing all the proper conditions in the house, for example, by elevating the south-west corner in some way.

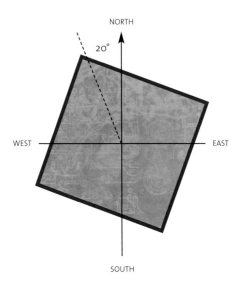

Misaligned house
This house is tilted, or misaligned, by 20° and steps need to be taken to try to correct the situation.

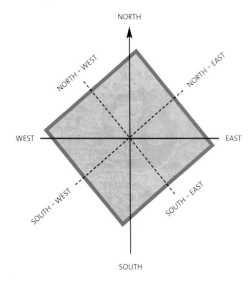

A rotated site
This house has rotated so that the cardinal points are now at the four corners. The same basic principles of Vastu apply.

New York: portrait of a city

Manhattan Island, in New York City, is now one of the most well-known urban landscapes in the world. Yet what would the Ancient Sages have thought of this city in terms of Vastu?

Most thriving cities are located near water, a symbol of prosperity; indeed, Manhattan is surrounded by water, with the Hudson River on one side and the East River on the other. The flow of water is predominantly from the north-west to south-east. According to Vastu the fact that the water flows from the west to the east is positive; however, because it also lows from north to south, it also indicates that prosperity flows out of New York as quickly as it flows in. Nonetheless, the city benefits from being near water, as the sea breeze blowing straight off the Atlantic Ocean helps reduce pollution.

One of the first things a vistor to New York will notice is the abundance of skyscrapers. Though these are not prevalent in India, any high buildings are seen as a symbol of aspiration, and there is certainly no shortage of ambition in New York. New York is also known as the Big Apple, clearly a symbol of prosperity.

The roads and the island itself are orientated along the north-east and south-west axes, with an extended north-east and south-west. The north-west and the south-east are depleted. This would indicate that activities related to the north-east and the south-west have become the main preoccupation for most New Yorkers. The south-east is the kitchen area of the home. Although New York has no shortage of food, most New Yorkers tend to eat out or order in,

The Manhattan skyline and the Hudson River

Seeing the Manhattan skyline for the first time can be an awe-inspiring experience. In Vastu the high skyscrapers are seen as symbols of aspiration and this particular skyline has been an inspiration to many artists and creative thinkers.

New York's grid system
New York city has been built following an intricate grid system, which is orientated to the compass directions—an ideal city for the practice of Vastu.

for cooking is not high on their list of priorities. Having a depleted north-west encourages restlessness, and therefore contributes to making New York into a city with an even more transient atmosphere.

The south-west is the direction connected to business and ancestry. This is where the thriving financial district is located, and is the oldest, most-developed area in the city. Many of the tallest buildings are also located in the south-west, making this area heavy and higher, which is an ideal situation for business prosperity. Ellis Island, situated in the south-west, is where many immigrants first entered America, thus giving this area a strong connection to the island's ancestry.

The north-east is the direction for the arts, learning, and spiritual knowledge. Historically New York has been home to many idealists, reformers, and religious leaders. It also has an abundance of museums and other cultural activities. This is the perfect counterbalance for the materialistic preoccupations associated with the south-west.

The other aspect in New York's favour is that the centre, the Brahma bindu, has been left open: Central Park, the lungs of the city, provides the perfect relief to the seemingly endless city landscape of concrete and steel.

Chapter four

Vastu at work

The same basic principles of Vastu apply to both residential and commercial properties. One of the prime objectives for using Vastu in the workplace is to ensure good management, as harmonious relations between employers and employees will always improve a company's performance.

In many situations there is no apparent reason why one business has major financial problems while another is booming. Customers may walk past and barely notice some stores and yet mysteriously be drawn into others. Whatever the scenario, it is always best to employ the services of an experienced Vastu practitioner. In certain circumstances he or she may recommend major structural changes or advise vacating a property. Although this may not appear to make sense financially, the initial investment is often essential for the future smooth running of the company. Because there is such a wide range of business activities, it is necessary to apply Vastu principles according to the scope of the business, and a good practitioner will tailor their recommendations to the individual needs of the company.

One of the most important factors for businesses is finding a suitable location. For example, businesses involved in administering medicine need to have a strong north-east aspect to charge the medicine with natural prana, which will make it more potent; those related to women's issues or women support groups will flourish with a strong south-east influence because Agni resides in the south-east and is known to protect the health of women.

Another essential aspect is the location of the different offices and departments in the business, such as the managing director's office or the accounts department. These considerations are dependent upon the size and the scale of the company. The physical needs of everyone involved in the business—from bathroom facilities and refreshment areas to the location of a canteen and details of access—must also be considered and properly designated. How the various rooms in the building are arranged with furniture and office equipment is also important.

Lakshmi

The Goddess of Fortune and embodiment of loveliness, grace, and charm, Lakshmi stands on a lotus with gold coins falling from her palms to symbolize prosperity. She is sometimes depicted on entrances to bring good luck and drive away evil.

If you work or run your own businesses from home it is necessary to have a specially designated area for this purpose. It is not a good idea just to clear a space on the kitchen table; indeed, having a specially demarcated area is an important preparation for the mind and you will find it easier to concentrate.

Directions and shapes

If the nature of your work is research or study, then the best part of the home to work in is the north. However, for other business purposes the ideal location is in the south-west area of the home. It is preferable if your designated room is a considerable distance from the main entrance of the house, so that you experience fewer disturbances. Your office should either be square or rectangular; if it is an irregular shape you can use screens or built-in cupboards to remedy the problem. If the room has a dual purpose as a bedroom and an office, it is best to place the bed in the south-west corner and keep your desk in the north-east corner of the room.

Your desk

Wherever your office is located, you should try to position the desk so that you face east or north while working, though you should ensure that it does not touch the north-east corner. The desk itself should be made of a good material such as wood or marble; try to avoid metal or plastic. Place the desk so that you will not be facing the wall when you look up, as it is much better to have an extended vista before you. Avoid having windows at your back, otherwise you will feel too exposed. A good seat is also essential, as it represents the lotus seat and needs to be fit for the gods. It should be a good height and well proportioned, with a high back for support.

Organizing your equipment

Like the rest of your home, the area where you work should be kept clean and organized to prevent the accumulation of stagnant energy. Keep filing cabinets to the south-west side of you. Computers or other electrical equipment, such as a photocopier, need to be positioned in the south-east section of the room. The wastepaper basket should be in the south-west and never in the north-east section.

Decorations

It is a good idea to have a small indoor water fountain in the north-east, for this keeps the room fresh and symbolizes abundance. Other images of wealth, such as Lakshmi, the Indian goddess representing fortune, or pictures of water, can be hung on the north or east walls. Freshly cut flowers make the room fragrant and are another symbol of abundance. A shade of yellow is a good colour to choose for the walls, as yellow is mentally stimulating and awakens the mind.

Layout for a home office

This office is basically a square, as recommended by Vastu experts, and the desk faces the eastern wall, in which there is a window. Filing and storage cabinets are kept to the south-west and the water cooler is situated in the north-east direction. The room is decorated a fresh yellow, to stimulate the mind and keep it alert.

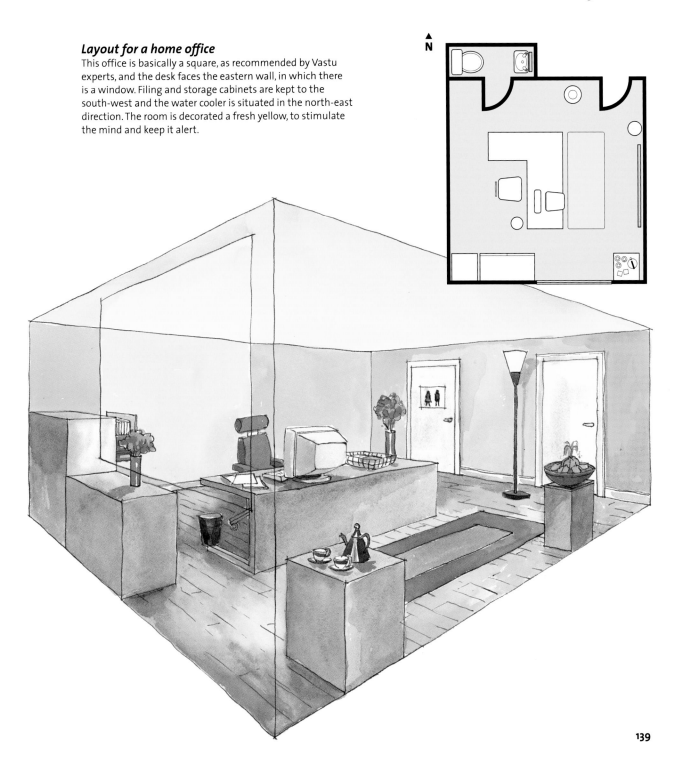

Choosing the right location to suit individual companies is very important: according to Vastu failure in business is attributed to the non-adherence to Vastu principles.

What kind of business?

Finding the right location for your offices depends upon the nature of the business. For example, shops need to be located where there is a high proportion of pedestrian traffic, whereas other specialist industries may need certain amenities readily available. Businesses of a similar nature tend to cluster together, in the financial district or the "rag trade" district, for example, as the cross-pollination of ideas in the direct competition of similar businesses helps them to flourish and grow.

Choosing materials

When looking for suitable premises the same principles that apply to apartment blocks also apply to businesses (see also pp.80-1). It is best to avoid complexes that are built of reinforced concrete or contain too much metal, as exposure to such material over a long period can cause major health problems.

If the business does not depend on retail, then it is better to avoid buildings at busy junctions or

Delhi
The financial district of Delhi (left) is spacious and has plenty of vegetation to encourage increased prosperity. This is the area of the city where financial businesses group together and can benefit from the cross-pollination of ideas.

Market stall
No matter what scale of business you have (see facing page), finding the right location is of great importance. Retail outlets need to be located where there is a high proportion of pedestrian traffic.

where four roads meet, on roundabouts, or at any other location that is too chaotic. A taller building or flyover should not overshadow the property. Likewise, avoid buildings with veedhi sholas pointing directly at them, such as roads or the sharp corners of other buildings (p.87). Ideally you should choose a building that is either square or rectangular and not one that is an irregular shape.

Many offices have multiple entrances. However, make sure that the main entrance is located in a positive direction, either in the north-east, the south of south-east, or the west of north-

west. There should be no obstructions to the main entrance and the door should sit squarely on its hinges and open easily, just as it should in a house (p.90).

Access

There must also be easy access to the building. If there is a car park allocated to the building, it should ideally be situated west or south of the premises. The gradient of the land surrounding the building should either be level or higher on the south or west side.

The reception area offers the first impression of a business: it is the buffer zone between the company and the outside world. The area should reflect the nature of the business, whether it is a waiting room at a dental surgery or the reception of a multinational corporation, and should be designed accordingly, giving an overall positive impression to visitors.

Locating reception

The location of the reception area in the building will obviously depend upon the position of the main entrance, as this is where visitors will expect to be welcomed. Because the reception area is the receiving zone of a business, it is ideally located in the north-east corner of the building, as prana flows in from the north-east. If the reception area is positioned in the north-east, it should, if possible, be at the lowest point, with either steps

or a lift leading up into the heart of the company.

The main reception desk should ideally be positioned in the south or west corner of the room (see diagram below), so that the receptionist faces either north or east. The person's back should be against the wall, to give a sense of protection, while the computer should be kept on the south-east section, or fire corner, of the main reception desk.

Improving the atmosphere

It is important to create an appropriate atmosphere in the reception. Too many reception areas are buried in the centre of a building and have no natural light or proper ventilation, both of which are essential to convey natural harmony in the company. If there is no alternative, then a collection of house plants or colourful freshly cut flowers will quickly improve an airless,

The best place for your reception is in the north-east corner of your office.

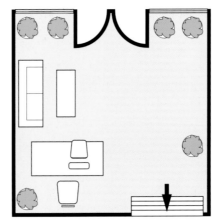

Plan for reception
The reception desk has been placed in the south-west corner. The receptionist has a clear view of any visitors coming in, while feeling protected by having a wall behind. The waiting area is located in the north-west area— the best area for the coming and going of visitors. The north-east has been left open, allowing for the free movement of prana.

windowless environment. The use of sound is equally important: harmonious sounds attract prosperity and wealth, so you should either play uplifting or soothing music or install a small indoor fountain, as the sound of running water is very pleasant and relaxing. Aquariums and small fish tanks can also provide a soothing, calming influence.

Appropriate furnishings

The furnishings chosen for the reception area also project the personality of a business: metal and glass portray an image of cold, intellectual efficiency and have a more masculine emphasis; wood is warmer and imparts a homelier, more caring, environment; dark wood, dim lighting, and richly patterned upholstery project a more serious and traditional image, one often found in political institutions and businesses that are older and well established.

Light, airy, and welcoming
This reception area is located in a central courtyard, with plenty of fresh air and light. There is greenery and water to provide a good atmosphere and the place feels efficient and well run.

Dark and foreboding
By contrast, this centrally located reception area is located away from natural light and, although house plants have been used to lighten the atmosphere, the prevailing feel is oppressive and cheerless.

The managing director of the company equates with the head of the household, according to Vastu principles. As such, the managing director's office corresponds to the master bedroom and should be one of the largest rooms, situated in the south-west corner of the building. The managing director's office should be away from the main entrance, providing greater protection and ensuring fewer disturbances.

The ancient Vastu texts take great heed of the direction you face while working, as practitioners believe it is fundamental to your state of mind. If you face east you will have peaceful and noble thoughts. Facing south-east, however, induces drowsiness and sleep. Facing south encourages a cruel, devious mind with determined thoughts and business deals. The south-west fosters a sinful and aggravated mind, while facing west is good for learning and play. Facing the north-west incites thoughts of travel and restlessness and facing north is good for spiritual development and accumulating knowledge. The north-east, however, is connected with transcendence and can be overwhelming, making you feel disconnected and otherworldly.

Ideally, the entrance to the office should be in the north-east quarter of the room. The desk needs to be positioned in the south or west of the room, allowing you to face east or north towards the doorway and be ready to receive people. It is disadvantageous to have your back to the door or a window, as you will feel more exposed and vulnerable. It is better to have a wall behind you for added support. Book shelves or closets should be along the west or south walls. A drinks cabinet or refreshment area can be located in the south-east corner of the room. If you have a safe, then that needs to be located along the north wall. Be careful which pictures you choose, as they can create a powerful impression (pp.120-1).

Services

If the business is large and has various administration departments, then these need to be properly located. General administration services connected to the business are best positioned in either the west or the south of the building on either side of the managing director's office. Make sure that the desks are positioned to enable staff either to face east or north.

The accounts department should be in the north of the building. Safes or valuables can also be kept in the north for added security, though the safe itself, because it is heavy, needs to be placed in the south or west. Even if your business is operating from just one room, you should carry out book-keeping in the north.

It is important that administration offices do not become overrun with paperwork, which causes energy to stagnate. To avoid this, supply good filing cabinets, which should be placed in the south or west, as they are heavy. It is also good to have an occasional clear-out to throw away unwanted old documents.

Refreshments

Whether it is a full-scale canteen for a large corporation or a just a snack machine, the refreshment area corresponds to the kitchen or dining area of a house. Cooking and refrigeration facilities equate with the kitchen, and should either be located in the south-east or the north-west. Water dispensers should be located in the north-east section of individual offices. However, a canteen or a restaurant in a hotel is equivalent to the dining area of a house and is best located in the west. Arrange tables so that staff face east or west as they eat. The atmosphere needs to be relaxed to aid digestion. One of the biggest problems about eating at work, especially if your job is stressful, is finding the time. It is important to have a change of environment, to be relaxed, and to allow at least ten minutes for digestion afterwards. Avoid eating at your desk, as this causes physical stagnation and can create health problems. It is better to have a light lunch to maintain constant energy level: if you eat heavy, tamasic food, red meat or too much starch, for example, you will feel drowsy in the afternoon.

The power office
Dark, wooden walls and furniture and dull colours contribute to a stuffy, foreboding atmosphere, where people might feel stifled or intimidated. The person in authority asserts themselves by using the imposing red leather chair as a prop.

The equipment needed for a company depends upon the nature of the business. However, whether it is a standard office or a large industry manufacturing a finished product certain similar rules will always apply.

If the business requires any heavy machinery such as printing equipment or photocopiers, then they and any other heavy items should be kept either in the south or west of the building. Similarly, heavy items that need to be kept throughout the premises, such as desks or heavy cabinets, should be positioned in the south-west of individual rooms. Any equipment relating to fire—boilers, welding tools, or kilns—needs to be placed in the south-east of the business. This also includes computers, for although they are a

modern invention and are not incorporated in the ancient wisdom of Vastu, modern Vastu practitioners group all electrical appliances under the fire element, relating to the south-east.

Wastepaper baskets should be placed in the south or west of the office, never in the north. The same applies to industries with large amounts of waste products, which should be disposed of in the south or west of the premises. Any finished products waiting to be dispatched can be stored in the north-west of the premises, which naturally imbibes a transitory energy. However, finished products that need to be stored for longer periods should be kept in the south-west. The north-east of any business should be free from heavy machinery, and should only be

Office equipment
Equipment in this office has been placed according to Vastu. The desks have been orientated so that employees face east, west, or north. Heavy equipment is situated in the south-west, while the toilet is in the north-west and the kitchen is in the south-east.

N

FILING CABINETS

WASTE

PHOTO-COPIER

KITCHEN AREA

used as a reception area or for other administrative offices.

Try to have as much natural light as possible throughout the premises: long-term exposure to fluorescent strip lighting destroys the internal balance of the physical body and can cause health problems. If the design of the building is such that natural light is unable to penetrate, install full-spectrum lighting (pp.104-5).

Bathroom facilities

The bathroom facilities in an office are comparable to the bathroom within the home and are therefore best located towards the south-west corner of the office building, the genital area of Vastu Purusha, or in the north-west. The bathroom should not open directly into the main office, but should be positioned away from it and have a separate entrance. There should also be separate bathrooms for men and women, so, if there is a problem with space, the women's bathroom can be positioned in the south-east corner of the building. However, if a bathroom is located in the north-east corner of the office, it will cause a drain on finances.

So much time is spent at work that, if possible, it should feel like a home away from home. It is a good idea to have shower facilities, as many people like to play sports at lunchtime or cycle into the office and need to freshen up before starting work. If the shower facility is separate from the bathroom, it can be located in the east.

The toilets should be kept in the south and west of the room, aligned along the north-south or east-west axis so that you face either north or east while sitting. The sinks and the shower can be along the north or east walls, though they should not touch the north-east corner. The moon influences bathrooms, so there should be some reflective surfaces, such as mirrors, and the lighting should not be harsh. Keep the room clean, fresh, and fragrant. Exposure to natural light is advisable to keep the room dry.

Protecting your finances
Kubera watches over the north of the building and is the protector of wealth, so this is the best area for any dealings with money, especially the accounts department.

The design currently in vogue for modern office spaces is the open-plan model, with employees being offered individual workstations. The workstations are often arranged in the form of a cross, with each employee sitting in a half cubicle. The idea behind this arrangement is to maximize space efficiency, to create a stimulating, competitive atmosphere, and to increase productivity. However, according to Vastu this paradigm has positive and negative implications.

Harnessing group energy and directing it towards a common goal works in theory, although in practice the open-plan approach usually works for some people and not for others. Certain personality types excel when working in privacy, while others prefer the energy of a group atmosphere. Instead of being stimulating, an open-plan office can be very distracting, especially when the dividing walls between compartments are low and there is no sense of privacy. Conversely, when the dividing walls are too high they can block the flow of natural light, which is equally essential for the well being of employees. Each individual situation has to be considered carefully to maximize the benefits and reduce negative influences.

According to Vastu, when the workstations are organized in the shape of a cross and aligned to the cardinal points, certain cubicles will have a more positive effect than others. Whoever is given the north-east corner will be forced to face either south or west, which can cause lethargy unless the desk faces away from the wall. This would be a good adjustment all round, as the wall then supports the back. The south-east compartment is fine provided the desk is positioned so that you are facing north. This position would be more advantageous for a woman than for a man as Agni resides in the south-east and is known to protect the health of women.

The person in the north-west compartment will suffer from restlessness and may not stay with the company long, so employees allocated this desk may come and go in quick succession. The south-west compartment is the best location for work and productivity. The other problem with workstations is that the employee's back is exposed, which can be very distracting, especially if there is a busy walkway behind.

Choice and flexibility

The best arrangement is to offer flexibility so that, without moving the workstation, the employee has the option of facing any direction. Movable screens are also important to allow different personality types to create their own individual environments and control the flow of light themselves. The workstations should be

Old and new
The traditional open-plan office (above) typically arranged all the workforce in a "schoolroom" pattern, with everyone facing the same direction. A more usual modern layout (facing page) is for workstations to form informal clusters and groups.

positioned more towards the south-west of the room, leaving the north-east corner clear.

Chairs have a big influence on posture and performance. Many people sit for up to eight hours at their desk, so a good chair is a great investment to avoid long-term back problems.

Photocopiers cause considerable disruption and are best in the south-east corner or in a separate room. It is also good to have fresh plants and flowers positioned around the office, as these will immediately improve the atmosphere.

Glossary

AGNI God of Fire, who resides in the south-east. Any equipment relating to fire, such as the cooker, hearth, or electronic equipment, should be located in the south-east. He is also known to protect the health of women in the house.

ANCIENT SAGES see **Rishis**

ARANYAKAS see **Vedas**

AYURVEDA Ancient system of healing from India derived from the **Vedas**, based on the understanding that a person's health depends upon the balance of the three **gunas** inherent in their constitution.

BALIDAANA A ritual performed before moving in to a new residence, whereby protective spirits are asked to enter and look after the new inhabitants.

BHAVA A particular state or mood induced by **rasa**, a strong sentiment or aesthetic experience.

BRAHMA One of the gods of the Hindu **triad** of **Brahma**, **Vishnu**, and **Shiva**. He is the symbol of creation and is connected with the origin and control of the universe. Brahma has four faces, three of which are normally visible. These represent the four **Vedas**, the four hands, and the four directions. He holds objects such as a rosary, a water pot, a book, and a lotus; his vehicle is a swan. **Saraswati** is his female counterpart.

BRAHMA BINDU The point at which the north-east and south-west lines cross on the **Sakala**. Heavy objects or masonry should be avoided in this area.

BRAHMANAS see **Vedas**

BUDHA Hindu name for Mercury. The closest planet to the sun and therefore the fastest, he is the messenger of the gods. A changeable and restless god, he is at his most active in the living or dining room.

CHANDRA Hindu name for the moon. She is the ruler of subconscious, instinctive activities, and presides over the bathroom. See also **Soma**.

CHARA VASTU One of the three bodies of **Vastu Purusha** that rotates throughout the year in accordance with the seasons. It rotates in a clockwise direction, resting for three months in one position. Different directions predominate according to the time of year. Vastu Purusha's third body or position is fixed above the earth. See also **Nitya Vastu**.

CHI Chinese name for the subtle energetic or magnetic forces that pervade any given space or living organism. How this vital energy circulates is vital for our well being. Compare with **prana**.

DURGA One of the most important Hindu goddesses, Durga is a powerful protectress. Of her many manifestations, one of her more benign forms is **Parvati**, wife of **Shiva**. **Kali** is one of her terrible incarnations. She has eight arms and up to three eyes. Her vehicle is a lion or tiger and she holds a snake, sword, club, bow and arrow, drum, wheel, and shield.

EPICS see **Mahabarata** and **Ramayana**

FENG SHUI Chinese art of geomancy believed to have its roots in **Vastu Vidya**. Like Vastu it aims to restore the balance between the home, the microcosm, and the movement of the cosmos, the macrocosm, by respecting the natural flow of cosmic energy.

FIVE ELEMENTS see **Maha Bhutas**

GANESH One of the most popular Hindu gods, he has an elephant's head, four to ten arms, and a rounded belly symbolizing the universe. He is the God of Wisdom and Fortune and the remover of obstacles. His vehicle is a rat and he usually holds his missing tusk, a rope, an axe, a goad, and a dish of sweets.

GARBHAGRIHAM Inner sanctum of a temple.

GARUDA Half-man, half-bird, this creature is the vehicle of **Vishnu** and king of the birds.

GNOMON A circular stake made of wood, such as ivory or sandalwood, that is fixed into the ground at the centre of a large circle and used to find true north.

GOPURA Sanskrit word for town gate or gateway, usually erected as an entrance to temple complexes, often reaching heights of up to 30 m (100 ft.).

GUNA There are three gunas, **sattva**, **rajas**, and **tamas**, which, together with their individual attributes, make up **prakritti**, the equivalent of what is known as nature in the West.

GURU Hindu name for Jupiter. He is known as the remover of darkness and represents wisdom, learning, and knowledge. Guru resides over the study or library but also watches over valuables.

HASYA One of the three **rasa** suitable for interior decoration. Hasya is comic.

INDRA King of Gods to whom the Vedic hymns are dedicated. A once-powerful god, he has now diminished in importance. He rides an elephant and brandishes a bolt of lightning, a lance, a sword, or a bow and arrow. He is associated with the east.

KALI A ferocious manifestation of the powerful goddess **Durga**, Kali, literally "the black one", who slays demons and protects the earth. Her skin is blue or black and she is often depicted as an old woman wearing a garland of skulls, whose tongue drips with the blood of her victims. **Nirtti**, Goddess of Darkness but also Lord of the Demons in her male manifestation, is associated with Kali.

KRISHNA, literally "the black one", is the eighth of the ten incarnations of **Vishnu**. He is often depicted as a young man playing a flute, with his right leg crossed in front of his left; his skin is usually black or blue. His vehicle is **Garuda**.

KUBERA Dwarf-like God of Wealth and Fame, whose fat belly betrays his affluence. He guards the north of any room or building, so this is where valuables should be stored.

KUJA Hindu name for the planet Mars, associated with fire and war. Kuja has an unstable, destructive nature and resides in the south-east, or **Agni**, quarter, the ideal location for the kitchen.

LAKSHMI is the popular Goddess of Wealth and Happiness. She is the wife of **Vishnu**, normally depicted standing on a lotus flower with golden coins falling from her palms to symbolize prosperity.

LODESTONE A form of magnetite rock with a pole at either end that repels and attracts the similar and opposite poles of other magnets respectively.

MAANA Perfect measurement or proportion.

MAHA BHUTAS The five natural elements, ether, earth, air, water, and fire.

MAHABARATA One of two great literary works to emerge between 400BC to AD600 recounting in epic form the rise and fall of the Kuru dynasty. The tales focus on the mythical inner battles that the children from this royal dynasty had to fight and the choices they made between good and evil. Compare with **Ramayana**.

MANDALA Takes the form of a square representing the earth and has eight compass directions: the major directions are north, south, east, and west, the minor directions north-east, north-west, south-east, and south-west. See also **Vastu Purusha Mandala** and **Sakala**.

MARMA STHANAS Points on the body of **Vastu Purusha** that are considered vulnerable, such as the heart, chest, navel, and genitals. Heavy objects or pillars should be avoided in these areas.

NIRTTI Goddess of Destruction but also Lord of the Demons and God of Misery and Destruction. Nirtti is associated with **Kali**, the ferocious aspect of the goddess **Durga**. In his male manifestation he resides in the south-west. Ghosts, poverty, gambling, sleep, and night wanderers fall into his realm. He stands upon a lion, a man, or a corpse holding a javelin, a shield, a staff, a sword, and teeth.

NITYA VASTU One of the three bodies of **Vastu Purusha** that moves in a 24-hour cycle. It rotates in a clockwise direction, resting for three hours in each of the eight positions. Different directions predominate according to the time of day. Vastu Purusha's third body or position is fixed above the earth. See also **Chara Vastu**.

PARAMASHAYIKA see **Vedic square**

PARVATI is the female manifestation of **Shiva** and is usually depicted with him, either standing beside him or seated on his knee. Together they represent the dual nature of the Absolute. See also **Durga**.

PRAKRITTI Cosmic creation, referred to in the West as nature, having three universal attributes in the form of the three **gunas**.

PRANA The Hindu name for the subtle energetic or magnetic forces that pervade any given space or living organism. The opposite of prana is said to be matter. How this energy circulates is vital for our well being. Compare with **chi**.

PRASAD Blessed food offered to gods before being distributed among the guests. This forms part of a series of rituals performed before taking up residence in a house. See also **puja**.

PRESERVING ZONE South-west corner of any building. This should always be blocked to prevent positive energies entering in the north-east from leaving.

PUJA Any ritual performed to a deity where vegetarian food, incense, or flowers are offered in their honour. A puja can be performed either at home or in public temples.

PURANAS written later than the **Vedas**, around the eighth century, these texts are stories based on individual gods, their spouses and children, their manifestations, and their incarnations.

RAJAS One of the three **gunas**; **sattva**, rajas, and **tamas**. Rajas manifests itself as action, change, and movement, and represents the energy moving between the two extreme poles of sattva and tamas. Rajas is influential in the south-east and north-west of any given space. **Brahma,** the creator, is associated with rajas.

RAMAYANA One of two great literary works to emerge between 400BC to AD600 devoted to Rama, the seventh incarnation of **Vishnu**. Historically the tales focus on the rise of the Aryan people, although they are also symbolic myths recounting acts of heroism, filial and matrimonial devotion, and battles of conscience. Compare with **Mahabarata**.

RASA One of nine strong sentiments or aesthetic experiences that give way to

bhava, a particular state or mood. The rasa recommended for interior decoration are **shingara**, **hasya** and **sahanta**, the seductive, the comic, and the peaceful.

REGENTS OF SPACE see **Vasus**

RIG-VEDA see **Vedas**

RISHIS or Ancient Sages were perceived as fathers of the human race. Seven in number, they are the authors of the **Vedas**.

SAHANTA One of the three **rasa** suitable for interior decoration. Sahanta is peaceful and meditative.

SAKALA The basic **Mandala** consisting of one square. This square represents earth, with the two poles, north and south, and the rising and setting of the sun in the east and west demarcating the earth's surface.

SARASWATI is the female counterpart of **Vishnu**. She is the Mother Goddess and a Goddess of Learning, Knowledge, and Wisdom. She rides a swan or peacock and carries items such as an arrow, a bell, a book, a bow, or a conch.

SATTVA One of the three **gunas**; sattva, **rajas**, and **tamas**. Sattva is the force of coherence, evolution, and growth and represents the positive, creative element. Sattva is influential in the north-east of any given space. **Vishnu**, the preserver, is associated with sattva.

SHANI Hindu name for the planet Saturn. Of the five influential planets in Vastu, Shani is the slowest-moving and also the darkest. He resides in all the dark areas of a house, in basements and

cupboards, for example.

SHINGARA One of the three **rasa** suitable for interior decoration. Shingara is seductive, induced by beauty.

SHIVA One of the gods of the Hindu triad of **Brahma**, **Vishnu**, and Shiva. Shiva is the creator and destroyer. He is usually depicted with a blue-painted throat and his sacred animal is Nandi, the bull. In his four hands he normally holds a bow, a club, a drum, and a noose. His symbol is the linga, or phallus, often accompanied by the female yoni. His female counterpart is the goddess **Parvati**.

SHUKRA Hindu name for the planet Venus. Shukra presides over the sensual side of human nature, including romance, passion, and beauty, and also influences the arts.

SOMA, also known as **Chandra**, is the nectar of the gods. He is connected with the north-east, the direction from which cosmic energy flows. For half the month, during the waning period of the moon, the gods feed on Soma to sustain their immortality. For the other half, when the moon is waxing, **Surya** replenishes Soma with water from the ocean.

SPACE DIRECTIONS The different directions of a compass that the **Ancient Rishis** considered to be active forces. These were explained as gods: **Kubera** in the north, **Indra** in the east, **Yama** in the south, and **Varuna** in the west; **Soma** was connected to the north-east, **Agni** to the south-east, **Vayu** to the north-west, and **Nirtti** to the south-west. See also **Vasus**.

SURYA Hindu name for the sun. He is

Lord of the East and resides in the north-east quarter of a room or building.

TAMAS One of the three **gunas**; **sattva**, **rajas**, and tamas. Tamas represents the power of inertia, atrophy, and dissolution and is therefore a destructive energy. Tamas is influential in the south-west of any given space. **Shiva** the destroyer is associated with tamas.

TANTRAS A series of ancient texts written between seventh and seventeenth centuries devoted to religious and magical practices, including ritual sexual acts, and focus on the fusion of opposites, the male and female.

TRIMURTI The Hindu triad, or trinity, of **Shiva**, **Vishnu**, and **Brahma**.

UPANISHADS See **Vedas**.

VARUNA is the Upholder of Universal Law connected to fate and unexpected events. He is associated with the north.

VASTU PURUSHA The "spirit" or "essence" representing the all-pervasive life force inherent throughout existence. Symbolized as a man with his head facing the earth, this image reminds us that every house behaves like a living organism. He lies with his head in the north-east, the direction from which all cosmic energy flows.

VASTU PURUSHA MANDALA A three-dimensional **yantra** used in Vastu to encapsulate all the forces acting on a given space. A Vastu practitioner organizes any area, large or small, according to this square.

VASTU SHAASTRAS Rules and regulations related to **Vastu Vidya**.

VASTU VIDYA literally means "dwelling science". It has its roots in Vedic philosophy, which emerged around 4,500 years ago, and aims to restore balance between the home, the microcosm, and the movement of the cosmos, the macrocosm, thereby bringing health, wealth, and happiness. Compare with **Feng Shui**.

VASUS The deities, or regents, of space presiding over each of the eight compass directions. Vasu literally means "that which surrounds". See also **Space directions**.

VAYU God of Wind, ruling over the north-west corner. He is described in the **Vedas** as being exceptionally good-looking, riding a deer, and carrying a white flag.

VEDAANGA Branch of the **Vedas** concerned with astrology.

VEDAS Dating from around 2500BC, the **Vedas** are the oldest Indo-European philosophical documents containing the foundation of Indian thought, culture, and sacred law. They are divided into three parts: the *Samhitas*, comprising the *Rig-Veda* (songs in praise of the gods), the *Sama-Veda* (melodies accompanying these songs), and *Yayur-Veda* (sacrificial formulae); the *Brahmanas*, which explain the significance of sacrifices and rituals; and the *Aranyakas* and *Upanishads*, which are philosophical and mystic writings discussing the nature of Highest Reality.

VEDHAS Any obstruction that restricts the flow of energy, such as a tree overshadowing a front door or a church opposite a main entrance.

VEDIC SQUARE, or Paramashayika. If the **Sakala** is divided into nine equal divisions on each side, it forms a diagram consisting of 81 squares. This is the Vedic square and is a visual form of the nine-times table, nine being a sacred number and attributed to one of the nine planets. This geometric representation of energy is a magic diagram and is known as a **yantra**. This square has been used by architects for thousands of years to create geometrical patterns and buildings.

VEEDHI SHOLA A road that runs directly towards a property. This can cause problems for the inhabitants.

VISHNU One of the gods of the Hindu triad of **Brahma**, Vishnu, and **Shiva**. Vishnu has ten major incarnations: Matsya, Kurma, Varcha, Narashima, Vamana, Prasurama, Rama, **Krishna**, Buddha, and Kalki. His female counterpart is **Lakshmi**. His animal is **Garuda**.

VISHWAKARMA, or Tvastri, is the Creator or Architect of the Gods. He normally holds various tools, a book, or a water jug.

YAMA God of Dharma and Death, who was the first mortal. He holds a club and rides a black buffalo or bull. He is associated with the south.

YANTRA Timeless diagram mapping cosmic energies active in any given space. Yantras can also be used to ward off harmful energies. See also **Vedic square**.

Bibliography

Acharya, Prasanna Kumar, **A DICTIONARY OF HINDU ARCHITECTURE**, Oxford University Press, London–New York, 1927

Acharya, Prasanna Kumar (trans.), **SILPAASTRA**, Oxford University Press, London–New York, 1933

Acharya, Prasanna Kumar, **INDIAN ARCHITECTURE ACCORDING TO MANASARA-SILPASASTRA**, Patna, distributed by Indological Book Corp., 1979

Bhattacharjee, Harish Chaudra, **A GUIDE TO ASTROLOGY**, Asis Bhattacharjee, Calcutta, 1967

Bhattacharyya, Tarapada, **A STUDY ON VASTUVIDYA OR CANONS OF INDIAN CULTURE**, Patna, 1948

Boner, A., Sarma, S. R., & Bäumer, B., **VASTUSUTRA UPANISHAD: THE ESSENCE OF FORM IN SACRED ART**, Motilal Banarsidass, Delhi, 1982

Braha, James. T., **ANCIENT HINDU ASTROLOGY FOR WESTERN ASTROLOGERS**, Hermetician Press, Miami, 1986

Chakrabarti, Vibhuti, **INDIAN ARCHITECTURAL THEORY: CONTEMPORARY USES OF VASTU VIDYA**, Curzon, Richmond, 1998

Chandra, Suresh, **ENCYCLOPAEDIA OF HINDU GODS AND GODDESSES**, Sarup & Sons, New Delhi, 1998

Chawla, Rakesh, **VAASTU**, Full Circle, New Delhi, 1997

Coomaraswamy, Ananda Kentish, **VISVAKARMA: EXAMPLES OF INDIAN ARCHITECTURE, SCULPTURE, PAINTING, HANDICRAFT CHOSEN BY A. K. COOMARASWANY**, published by the author, London, 1914

Danielou, Alain, **THE GODS OF INDIA**, Inner Traditions, New York, 1985

Flood, Gavin, **AN INTRODUCTION TO HINDUISM**, Cambridge University Press, Cambridge, 1999

Harle, J. C., **TEMPLES AND GATEWAYS IN SOUTH INDIA: THE ARCHITECTURE AND ICONOGRAPHY OF CIDAMBARAM GOPURAS**, Munshiram Manoharlal, New Delhi, 1995

Jansen, Eva Rudy, **THE BOOK OF HINDU IMAGERY: THE GODS AND THEIR SYMBOLS**, Binkey Kok Publications BV, Diever, 1998

Johari, Harish, **NUMEROLOGY: WITH TANTRA, AYURVEDA, AND ASTROLOGY**, Destiny Books, Rochester, c.1990

Kramrisch, Stella, **THE HINDU TEMPLE**, Motilal Banarsidass, Delhi, 1976

Krishna Das, P., **THE SECRETS OF VASTU**, Udayalakshmi Publications, Secunderabad, 1989

Mayamuni (trans. Bruno Dagens), **MAYAMATA**, Sitaram Bhartia Institute of Scientific Research, New Delhi, distributed by Indian Book Centre, 1985

Middleditch, Michael, **THE NEW YORK MAPGUIDE: THE ESSENTIAL GUIDE TO MANHATTAN**, Penguin, London–New York, 1998

Mishra, Dr S. P., **THE MIRACLES OF COLOUR THERAPY: A GUIDE TO DRUGLESS SYSTEM OF MEDICINE IN HEALTH AND DISEASE**, Firma KLM Private Ltd., Calcutta, 1995

Mitchell, A. G., **HINDU GODS AND GODDESSES**, UBSPD, Delhi, 1998

Moorty, K. K., **THE ABODES OF GODS AND PILGRIMS**, Tirupati, Message Publications, 1989

Moynihan, Elizabeth, B., **PARADISE AS A GARDEN IN PERSIA AND MUGHAL INDIA**, G. Braziller, New York, 1979

Muralidhar Rao, D., **VAASTU SHILPA SHAASTRA**, S. B. S. Publishers, Bangalore, 1995

Muralidhar Rao, D., **TREASURE TROVE AND MORE: VAASTU SHILPA SHAASTRA**, Galgotia Publications, New Delhi, 1997

Pandurangi, K. T. (trans. Sri Madhvacharya), **UPANISHADS. TAITTIRIYOPANISHAD**, Sriman Madhva Siddhantonnahiri Sabha, Tirupati, 1990

Paranjpe, V. G. (trans.), **ABEL BERGAIGNE'S VEDIC RELIGION**, Motilal Bandarsidass, Delhi, 1978

Poynder, Michael, **PI IN THE SKY: A REVELATION OF THE WISDOM TRADITION**, Rider, London, 1992

Prabhavananda, Swamy & Manchester, Frederick (trans.), **THE UPANISHADS**, Vendanta Press, Hollywood, & Ramakirshna Vedanta Centre, Bourne End, 1983

Puri, Dr. P. P., **APPLIED VASTU IN MODERN ARCHITECTURE**, Vastu Gyan Publications

Radice, Betty (ed.), **HINDU MYTHS**, Penguin Books, London–New York, 1975

Raichur, Pratima, **ABSOLUTE BEAUTY: RADIANT SKIN AND INNER HARMONY THROUGH THE ANCIENT SECRETS OF AYURVEDA**, HarperCollins, New York, 1997

Raja Rao, Ar. K. V., **SCIENCE IN VASTU APPLICATIONS**, WAVES, Bangalore, 1995

Rama Rao, M., **TEMPLES OF TIRUMALA, TIRUPATI, AND TRICHANUR**, Devasthanams, Tirupati, 1982

Randhawa, Mohindar Singh, **BEAUTIFUL TREES AND GARDENS**, Indian Council of Agricultural Research, New Delhi, 1961

Sarasvati, Satya Prakash (trans.), **ATHARVAVEDA**, Veda Pratishthana, New Delhi, 1992

Sen, Chitrabhanu, **A DICTIONARY OF VEDIC RITUALS**, Concepts Publishers, Delhi, 1978

Shil-Ponde, **HINDU ASTROLOGY (JOYTISHA SHASTRA)**, Larwood Publishers, New York, 1939

Shukla, Dvijendra Nath, **ROYAL PALACE AND ROYAL ARTS**, Vastuvanmaya-Prakasna-Sala, Lucknow, 1967

Singh, Dharam Vir, **HINDUISM: AN INTRODUCTION**, Travel Wheels, Jaipur, 1995

Stutley, Margaret, **THE ILLUSTRATED DICTIONARY OF HINDU ICONOGRAPHY**, Routledge & Kegan Paul, London–Boston, 1985

Taluqdar of Ouhd (trans.), **PURANAS**, Matsyapurana, A. M. S. Press, New York

Vagbhata, **ASTANGASANGRAHA**, Chaukhambha Orientalia, Varanasi, 1995-6

Varahamihira (trans. Iyer, N. C.), **THE BRHAT SAMHITA OF VARAHA MIHIRA**, Sri Satguru Publications, Delhi, 1987

Viraraghavacharya, T. K. T., **HISTORY OF TIRUPATI**, Tirupati: Tirumala-Tirupati, Devasthanams, 1977

Many of the rare titles cited above are available through the New York Public Library (tel. (212) 930-0830) or the British Library in London (tel. +44 (0)20 7412 7000). You can browse databases listing their collections at their respective web sites, www.nypl.org/index.html and www.bl.uk. Yale University also hosts a worldwide listing of public libraries and other useful links at www.library.yale.edu/pubstation/libcats.html.

Index

Main entries are in **bold**.

Publisher's acknowledgements
Gaia Books would like to thank the following individuals for their help in the production of this book: Pie Chambers and Sunil Sethi of India Link; Emma Meysey-Thompson; the staff at Star Publishers/Distributors, 112 Whitfield St, London W1P; Chelsey Fox; Catherine Rockwood; Sara Mathews

Author's acknowledgements
I would like to acknowledge my debt and gratitude to Dr Subramanya Babu for accepting me as his student and for sharing his great insight and wisdom. I also extend many thanks to Shri Pattabhi Jois for planting my feet firmly on the right path. Thankyou to Brenda Pegrum for all her help and assistance on this project.

For further information on private consultations and forthcoming workshops you can contact the author at julietpegrum@vastuvidya.com

Photographic credits
Achim Bedrich colllection, Munich (Astrogram, Rajasthan 19th century, guache on paper) 23
AKG London/Erich Lessing 120, 121
Axiom (David Constantine) 127
Tim Beddow/The Interior Archive (owner: Moore) 102, 116
Fernando Bengoechea/The Interior Archive (owner: Schwartz) 100
Michael Dunne/ www.elizabethwhiting.com 143T
Jo Godfrey Wood 1, 128, 141
Robert Harding Picture Library 10, 11, 12, 14-15, 42, 43, 53, 61, 64, 68-9, 72, 77, 80, 83, 118, 135, 140, 148, 149
Robert Harding Syndication (Inspirations ©. GE Magazines Ltd) 95T, 110
Rodney Hyett/ www.elizabethwhiting.com 95B
Cecilia Innes/The Interior Archive (artist: Erik Bendsten) 106
National Museum of India, New Delhi/Bridgeman Art Library, London 45
Michael Nicholson/ www.elizabethwhiting.com 143B
Jamie Marshall/Tribal Eye 21, 88, 91
Anne and Bury Peerless 44, 66, 67
Juliet Pegrum 20
Fritz von der Schulenburg/The Interior Archive (designer: Anokhi, Jaipur, India) 46, and (designer: Stephanie Hoppen) 144, and (Mallinson/Private Hong Kong) 124
Sporting Pictures 76
Christopher Simon Sykes/The Interior Archive (artist: Edwina Sandys) 117
Henry Wilson/The Interior Archive (designer: Stephen La Grange 114

The publishers have made every effort to credit all contributors. In the event of an omission or error, corrections will be made in subsequent editions.

The Feng Shui Handbook

Master Lam Kam Chuen ISBN 1 85675 047 7 £12.99
Adjust your living and working environments using the principles of feng shui and enjoy the benefits of a healthier, more fulfilling life.

The Personal Feng Shui Manual

Master Lam Kam Chuen ISBN 1 85675 053 1 £12.99
How to adjust your personal routine according to the five animals and elements system – to create more health, wealth and happiness.

The Feng Shui Kitchen

Master Lam Kam Chuen and Lam Kai Sin ISBN 1 85675 170 8 £12.99
Design your kitchen and cooking habits to obtain the most from your food. Includes delicious Chinese recipes for every season.

Heart and Home

Beverly Pagram ISBN 1 85675 054 X £14.99
A design source book inspired by nature's elements and seasons, for creating sensual, spiritual surroundings.

Natural Housekeeping

Beverly Pagram ISBN 1 85675 034 5 £9.95
Rediscovered recipes that kept households gleaming before chemical cleaners. Plus natural ways to scent and decorate your home.

H is for ecoHome

Anna Kruger ISBN 1 85675 030 2 £4.99
An A-Z of household chemicals, indoor pollutants, and how to avoid them.

To order a book or request a catalogue contact:
Gaia Books Ltd, 20 High Street, Stroud, Glos GL5 1AZ
T: 01453 752985 F: 01453 752987 E: info@gaiabooks.co.uk

visit our web site to see a complete list of our titles: www.gaiabooks.co.uk